Fatwa

Living with a Death Threat

Jacky Trevane

Hodder & Stoughton
LONDON SYDNEY AUCKLAND

Copyright © 2004 by Jacky Trevane

First published in Great Britain in 2004

The right of Jacky Trevane to be identified as the Author of the Work has been asserted by her in accordance with the Copyright, Designs and Patents Act 1988.

10 9 8 7

British Library Cataloguing in Publication Data
A record for this book is available from the British Library

ISBN 9780340862421

Typeset in Goudy by Avon DataSet Ltd,
Bidford on Avon, Warwickshire

Printed and bound in Great Britain by
Bookmarque Ltd, Croydon, Surrey

The paper and board used in this paperback are natural recyclable products made from wood grown in sustainable forests. The manufacturing processes conform to the environmental regulations of the country of origin.

Hodder & Stoughton
A Division of Hodder Headline Ltd
338 Euston Road
London NW1 3BH
www.madaboutbooks.com

For Chloe

Contents

Prologue

It is time.

I have been waiting a long time for the right moment, the right way, the right reason. I am sitting at home, watching the sunlight stream through the open window, swamping and surrounding my beautiful, tiny granddaughter, until she dislodges her sunhat and scrunches up her baby eyes against its glare. I rescue her, of course, and snuggle her closely. I bury my head into her crinkly neck and cover her with kisses until she collapses into giggles. That wonderful, seductive baby smell. The smell my own babies had, talcum powdery, fresh, new, somehow innocent, unscathed . . .

Read my story, darling Chloe. When you are older, read my story and know that there is nothing as strong as a mother's love for her children, even though sometimes, no matter how hard you try, it just doesn't seem to be enough.

Your mother, my first daughter, is now in charge of her own destiny. Your aunt, my second daughter, has just turned eighteen years of age and can finally claim an identity and tell the world that she exists – officially.

I have waited fifteen long years and now I know.

Yes, it is time.

1

On the Run

It is time. In the shadowy light of dawn, I watch the hour hand reach five, and slip quietly out of bed. Bending down, so close that I can feel his breath on my cheek, I watch my husband's face as he sleeps. Curled up in slumber with one arm slung out over the end of the bed, his face is gentle, relaxed, innocent.

I tiptoe out of the bedroom to wake the girls. Everything is ready; Leila's school uniform on the back of the chair, Amira's clean clothes and a doll to play with. As they clamber out of bed to start the day, I put my finger to my lips and they are both instantly alert and conscious of the noise they are making. They too tiptoe around, preparing for school.

We must not wake Papa. If Papa wakes up he will be angry with us. My heart is beating fast and loud. I pray silently that he will sleep through the morning. Already the sounds of a new day begin to drift through the shutters: the grating and creaking of wooden wheels as donkeys drag carts along the dusty street, people on bicycles ringing their bells, the women at the local tap gossiping.

Within ten minutes we are ready to leave. I gather Amira up

into my arms, put my school bag over my shoulder, and turn to look for the final time, at the life we are leaving behind.

The whole of our lives had been contained in that flat: two carpets, a filthy, flea-ridden three-piece suite, a cooker, water in the taps most days, a water heater and a black-and-white TV. It had taken such an enormous amount of effort to accumulate and it would all have been worth it, but for the brute on the bed.

I was wasting valuable time I realised, as I stole another minute to examine my husband's features. This man, once the best husband a girl could wish for, was now a stranger. He awoke every morning, confident that he could treat us exactly how he liked when he liked, and knowing that there was nothing we could do about it. Well, there was something we could do, and now I was going to try to do it. Yet if he woke up too soon, if he realised we were gone, he would go mad. He would track us down and kill us. I had no doubt of that.

In the heat of the early morning, I shuddered, kissed Amira and, with a last brief glance at his face, closed the door as we made our way noiselessly down the four flights of shadowy stairs and out into the blinding sunlight that was the street.

'Look down, act normally. Like a Moslem wife should,' I reminded myself.

Though still early morning, the heat of the sun slammed into us. As we passed a woman sitting in the dust outside her doorway, I panicked, convinced she must be able to hear my heart beating. I muttered a greeting in Arabic, feeling the sweat begin to run down my cheeks. 'Come on, come on, hold it together, girl. You've only just left the flat. There's an awfully long way to go yet. Get a grip.'

We passed the communal water tap and Leila ran up to chat to one of the girls clinging to her mother's black robe as she filled a bucket. Amira and I continued on to the top of the street and round the corner, walking slowly to disguise the sense of urgency rippling through every bone in my body.

With a wave to the girls, Leila ran to catch us up. She was looking this way and that for the school bus, which usually waited at the top of the street, signalling us with three loud blasts of the horn.

But today, the school bus was not waiting. Where the bus normally stood was a little grey car. I could do nothing to prevent a smile escaping, for a moment breaking my mask of indifference. But I was immediately back in control as I casually approached the car and motioned for the girls to get in.

'Everything okay?'

'So far, so good.'

The relief began to flood through me as Jill threw me a reassuring smile from the driver's seat and we zoomed off to the bus station.

'Where's the bus? Has it broken down? Are you taking us to school, Jill? Where are Jack and Sheila?'

'They're still at home, Leila, getting ready for school. I'm taking you to the station.' She looked meaningfully at me. 'The bag is down there.'

She indicated under the passenger seat. I pulled the bag out and set it upon my knee. Such an unobtrusive, ordinary, black barrel bag – with the rest of our lives tucked inside it.

'It's happening, it's actually happening.' The thought raced through my mind over and over again, as I unzipped the top and took out a skirt and T-shirt.

'Come on darling, slip these on. How would you like to go on holiday and give school a miss?'

'Where to, Mama?'

I realised that Leila had discarded her uniform and was already pulling the T-shirt over her head. She was six now and ready for adventure.

'Well, Nanna and Grandad are taking a short holiday in Israel, and that's right next door to us here in Egypt. So I thought we'd bunk off school, not tell Papa and go to see them. What do you think?'

The car rounded a corner and the bus station came into view. My heart began to pound once more, as Leila asked, 'Mama, do we have to come back?'

Jill leaned over and whispered in my ear, 'The return bus tickets are in the side pocket, with your passport and $60 as agreed. Good luck, Jacky. You can do this.'

We hugged and kissed briefly, Jill wiping away a tear, me reluctant to leave the security and peace inside of the car. A minute later we were waving her off, three solitary figures on the dusty roadside with a doll and a small black holdall. It was still only six o'clock. The bus out of Cairo left at half past. It was a five-hour journey across the desert to the Israeli border, so before approaching the bus station, I stopped at a barrow on the side of the street and bought a kilo of tangerines. From a kiosk I bought two bottles of water and some processed cheese triangles that Amira loved. From the black bag I pulled a headscarf and quickly covered my long blonde hair which I had swept up into a tight bun that morning to avoid attracting undue attention. It was important to look as much like a dutiful Moslem wife and mother as possible for the plan to succeed. Taking Leila's hand, I crossed the road to the bus station.

There was an overriding smell of urine inside the tiny ticket office. A small but very rotund man was sitting behind an old, scratched desk, chatting loudly with three other men. There were three glasses of black tea on a tin tray, and a fan whirring away in the corner. Flies were crawling along the dusty window and walls.

He greeted us in Arabic. 'Good morning. Come in, come in here,' as he shouted at his colleagues to make room for the three of us. One of the men picked up Amira to admire her.

'Thank you. Good morning,' I replied, making sure to keep my head respectfully inclined as I handed over the tickets. As the man inspected them, I noticed two flies collide and land on the rim of his glass of tea. They crawled inside as he held the tickets up with one hand and grasped the glass firmly with the other. I took back the tickets as he slurped noisily from the glass.

'Your husband is not travelling with you?' he asked, wiping the tea from his chin with the back of his hand.

'He must work, unfortunately, but he will be able to collect us on our return, God willing,' I lied.

'God willing,' he replied, as I retrieved Amira and we made our way towards the bus.

'Find a seat near the back,' I urged, as Leila got on ahead of me. I wanted to be as unobtrusive as possible, to melt quietly into the background. Fortunately, there was a seat for everyone. This vehicle was far more modern than the old buses that wobbled around the city, overloaded with passengers and belching out frequent blasts of black smoke. This was a coach, and it was easier to maintain a degree of privacy.

Once in our seats, Amira sat happily with two cheese triangles, feeding one to her doll, of course. She never left her doll out of any activity, if at all possible. At two years old, she was a generally happy child, easily pleased, and at that moment in time I was immensely grateful for that.

Leila reached up and pulled one of the brown curtains across the far end of the window to block the glare of the sun. 'Will we see Nanna soon?' she asked eagerly.

'Yes, darling. But not many papas let their wives and children travel without them, and so some people may ask us questions because Papa is not with us. If they do, I want you to promise me not to say anything, even if I say some things that may not be completely true. It's because we want to see Nanna, and I don't want anyone to send us back. Do you understand?'

'Yes. We're moving, Mama, the bus is moving.'

My stomach lurched along with the coach as it began its fight with all the other vehicles and their horns. We were off at last. But would we make it all the way?

2

From Egypt to Israel

Once out of the city, the road was straight and narrow, stretching for miles. The scenery was fascinating to me. It was as if we were embarking on a journey back in time. There were lots of palm trees, occasional plots of land that were farmed, and traders standing with their barrows at the roadside, selling watermelons or tomatoes.

Every so often we passed a small village or settlement. The houses were made from rough brick and mud as in biblical times. Women dressed from head to toe in black walked barefoot with huge water carriers on their heads. They supported these giant clay urns with just one hand, holding a baby with the other. I could see thick, navy-blue tattoos decorating their arms and they wore many gold bangles around their wrists. Children with unkempt hair and dirty, bare feet were running about, flies buzzing around their heads. There was also a cattle-driven well with a man in a dirty *galabeya* regularly whipping the blindfold beast to keep it moving.

Gradually these intermittent signs of civilisation gave way completely to the vastness of the desert. Amira fell asleep and

Leila watched the desert fly by, mesmerised by the unending sea of sand stretching into the distance.

But I couldn't relax. I checked the black bag, counting the dollars, examining the passport and making sure they were still there. I fingered the piece of paper with the name of the hotel in Israel on it, imagining we were walking up the steps to the reception right now. Finally, I tucked the return section of the bus tickets in with the dollars, and was about to close the bag, when I froze. Someone was looking right at me, watching everything.

'Give these to your daughters. Your little one wanted a sandwich, didn't she? Cheese – we have enough, thanks be to God.'

An Egyptian woman, her head uncovered, caught my glance and smiled. She then held out a brown paper bag and offered it to me for the children. She spoke rapidly in Arabic, but then noticed my hair under the scarf. 'Are you American?' she asked.

I smiled and nodded, finally accepting the sandwiches and offering her some tangerines. This was not a wise thing to have done, I discovered, as she then took this as an invitation to sit and talk.

Many well-educated women in Egypt choose not to cover their heads with veils or scarves. They take care with their hairstyles and pay great attention to their make-up and nails. This woman's make-up was immaculate, in total contrast to that of poorer Moslem women. Black kohl had been delicately applied, with eyeshadow and foundation, finished off with burgundy lip liner, framing full, red lips. Poorer women applied kohl very thickly all around their eyes. Her nails were perfectly manicured, and her black hair was cut into a short, modern style.

Such was the degree of nervous tension running through me, I had failed to make these observations about her until it was too late. She began asking question after question in English now. As I'd lied about being American in the first place, it was then doubly difficult to dream up more lies that were feasible.

Her name was Mona and she was travelling alone. She paid a lot of attention to Leila, making her laugh and tickling her. Leila, with half a sandwich inside her, was obviously warming to the woman.

'I'm six and my little sister is two. But she's only just two and I'm nearly six and a half. We're going to see our Nanna.'

I wasn't angry, merely exasperated. Leila was a friendly child, and for the moment had forgotten about our little chat earlier. It wasn't hard to draw her into conversation usually. 'A cheese sandwich and she'll tell you her life story,' I thought.

This was stress that I could definitely do without. In desperation, I nudged Amira awake, gave her a drink and offered her a sandwich.

'Thank you for the sandwiches, Mona. I need to rest now, so we will speak later, yes?'

Mona smiled. 'Of course. If the little one wants, she can sit with me while you rest. I will tell her stories.'

'Maybe later, thank you.'

Mona stood up and reluctantly returned to her seat. I immediately pulled the scarf right down to cover every bit of my hair.

'Why did you say you were from America, Mama?'

'Sssh, darling. We don't want anyone to know anything about us. We just want to get to Nanna. I know it's hard for you to understand now, but you'll see why later, I promise.'

I put a reassuring arm around both my daughters and hugged them to me. I was so terrified of what we were doing that I needed their comfort and trust more than ever. I pretended to sleep, but Amira was restless, so we passed the time dressing and undressing dolly.

About a mile from the border, in the middle of the desert, there were buildings along the side of the road. Soldiers in green uniforms were standing around, armed with bayonets on their rifles, which were glinting in the sun. There were a couple of coffee shops, with tables outside where men were playing *tavla*, or backgammon. Inside, I could make out two old men smoking bubble pipes.

There was a lot more traffic – lorries, coaches, white Peugeots (the standard passenger hire cars), private cars. The coach veered off to one side and stopped. We were told to collect our entire luggage and take it with us into the building to buy our exit visas to leave Egypt. This was it. I had been rehearsing possible questions and answers in colloquial Arabic over and over in my head. Now it was for real.

We got off the coach, but I hung back to take a drink from the bottle of water. My throat was dry and my hands clammy, but then it was a sweltering day, so that was nothing unusual. I looked back across the desert. There was still such a long way to go.

Inside the building, I scanned the desks set up behind iron grilles, where men were issuing visas. People were paying up and moving on. The men stamping the visas looked bored and were chatting across their desks as they worked.

I chose carefully: an elderly, senior-looking man with a smile on his face. He was the most approachable, and we waited about ten minutes in his line.

I held my breath as I handed over our passport and bent down to pick up Amira.

'Peace be upon you, madam,' he stated without looking up, peering down at the passport.

'And on you, sir,' I replied quietly.

He was instantly more alert and attentive as he studied my dark-blue British passport. The people who had passed through before me had all been Egyptian, and he had begun to speak to me as if I were too. He was obviously surprised at the correctness of my form of address and, as a result, more interested in us. This was exactly what I had hoped wouldn't happen.

He held out his hand. 'The other one, if you please.'

'I'm sorry?'

'Your husband's passport. It is written here in your passport that you are married to an Egyptian national. Of course you are travelling with him, are you not?'

'Unfortunately not, sir. His work has prevented him from travelling with us this time.'

'Mama, mama, I need the toilet.' Leila tugged at my skirt.

'Just a minute, darling. We'll go together when I've finished here.'

'Is anyone accompanying you – an uncle, perhaps?'

'No sir, not this time. It is only a short trip, just two days in fact, to see my parents.'

The man leaned forward to examine Leila more closely. 'It is a problem for you travelling alone with two little ones. It is most unusual.' He paused, as if mulling something over, stroking his chin as his gaze wandered slowly over us.

'Look down. Stay calm. Raise your eyes very slightly and smile a little – not too much. Gently does it. Now, wipe the sweat very slowly from your face. Not too fast, don't give anything away.' I was mentally yelling to myself as we waited.

Suddenly, the man put down the visa stamp and picked up the telephone.

'Oh, God, he's not going to let us out! What is he going to do? What will happen to us? Should we make a run for it? What had the British Embassy said? "Don't turn back, whatever you do."'

The consul at the embassy had spelt out very clearly the possible consequences for us if we did not make it and had to return to Egypt. It was a very serious offence to take a man's children away from their father. I would be killed and the girls closely guarded until they were married off at an early age of maybe thirteen or fourteen. Even if I managed to get away, we would have to be very careful to stay hidden from him for the rest of our lives. My husband had the right to have a fatwa issued against me for my crime. A fatwa is the Islamic right to have someone killed, a death sentence. In leaving with the children, I would commit a sin against Islam and should not be allowed to live. The enormity of the risk I was taking suddenly dawned on me as I stood there.

My mind was racing, as the man shouted angrily into the phone and then slammed it down. It wasn't working. One of the few reasons I loved Egypt at that moment was the unreliability of their telecommunications system.

I wondered why he was so angry. I had chosen him because he looked so amenable and pleasant.

'Hesham!' the man suddenly yelled. Immediately a young man with a frightened look in his eyes appeared at his side. He wore brown trousers with a creased, beige, short-sleeved shirt.

The man turned his back on us and they spoke quietly together. Then he pointed at Leila, while Hesham nodded.

'A plan, I need a plan,' I thought desperately.

'You stay here,' he said, 'Hesham will take your pretty daughter to the toilet.'

I shrank back, putting a protective arm around Leila. 'I'm sorry, sir, but we are a Moslem family, and I will not allow her to go anywhere alone with a male. I will take her in a little while, God willing.'

'So!' he exclaimed. 'You are Moslem. Peace be upon you.'

'And upon you, sir,' I replied demurely.

'Hesham, bring Iman to sort out this little problem.'

13

A girl appeared from a doorway behind the desks, wiping her hands on her long skirt as she came towards us. She greeted me and offered to take Leila to the toilet. As I let her go, I had an idea. 'If there is a problem, then I have my husband's telephone number at work. He will be happy to answer any queries you may have.'

I foraged in my bag, as if searching for the number. Instead, I took out my purse. I pushed fifty piastres through the grille towards him. 'Could you reward Iman with this, please?'

I took a deep breath and pushed two five-Egyptian-pound notes through. Enough for a hundred phone calls. 'And this is for you to cover the cost of the phone call.'

He sat there looking unwaveringly at me for several long moments, as his fingers closed over the money. I continued to look down at the desk. I could feel his eyes boring into me.

Iman returned with Leila. He handed over her tip and she looked delightedly at me before scuttling away.

'Thank you for your concern, sir. We are most grateful.' I almost looked up at him, stopping at his nose, before lowering my gaze again quickly. I could feel him looking at us once more. He knew what was happening. A British woman was giving him money to let her out of the country with her children. He should make that call and contact the husband. But what difference did it make to him? It was certainly enough *baksheesh* to keep his mouth shut. He pocketed the cash, wet the stamp on the inkpad, and stamped the passport with exit visas.

'It was no trouble at all, madam. You have two beautiful daughters. Have a pleasant trip. You need to pay thirty-one pounds, fifty piastres for the visas. Peace be upon you.'

I counted out the money and handed it over. I had brought fifty Egyptian pounds with me and now I had six pounds and a few piastres left. For the moment, I was too excited and relieved to worry about the money, even though it had taken me many, many months to accumulate, hiding it away a few notes at a time. We had done it. We had managed, against all odds, to get out of Egypt, and I just could not wait to get back on that bus.

And suddenly we were walking away, out of the building, into the sunshine, looking for the bus. But the bus was not there. A lorry was parked in its place, and behind it was a stream of other vehicles.

Surely the bus could not have left without us? Would I be able to find another one to take us into Israel? For six Egyptian pounds? That wouldn't even cover the tip.

'You stupid, senseless idiot,' I chastised myself. 'Oh so clever, masterminding your little plan in there. Well, it took too long, didn't it? And now we're stuck in this hellhole!'

I could feel the panic rising in me. I clutched my throat and had to rush back across to the side of the building where I heaved and retched, until there was nothing left in my stomach.

The bus had gone without us, and we were stuck between countries with no money. I had no idea what to do next.

3

Across the Border

My scarf had fallen off into the dust. Wearily, I bent down to retrieve it, spitting into the dust to remove the revolting taste of vomit in my mouth. I really needed a drink. As I gazed upward, Leila's worried little face came into view, and I felt a pang of guilt. I had lost control there for a moment. I had to be stronger for their sakes.

From a distance I could hear someone calling urgently, 'Hello, hello.' I squinted in the direction of the voice to see who was calling.

Then Leila turned and smiled. 'Mama, it's the lady again. So we can't have missed the bus.'

She ran up and took Mona's hand, who was surprised and delighted.

'The bus has gone that way.' She indicated down a long, dusty track bordered by high fences. There were circles of barbed wire stretching all the way across from one fence to the other.

'We must walk now – this way.' I looked over to where she was pointing. There were people with their children and baggage making their way on foot along another track, bordered by tall, wire fences with ominous barbed wire strung along the top in large circles.

So this was the actual border. One side Egypt, the other Israel. Armed soldiers were everywhere, some with their guns slung casually over their shoulders, others standing to attention, guns poised in front of them. It felt almost surreal, in the middle of the desert, with the sand stretching out to the distant horizon beneath the brilliant sky.

'Thank you,' I smiled and nodded at Mona. 'But there's something I'd like to do first. It won't take long.'

I bent down and whispered in Leila's ear, pressing the remaining Egyptian money into her hand. She ran immediately to a battered old freezer standing outside the visa building. Iman was there, selling cold drinks. She handed four bottles of Coke in a used plastic bag to Leila. After quite a lengthy conversation, Leila returned.

'She said, "May God go with us", Mama, and she took all the money.'

I smiled. Two decent tips in one day. Iman must be one happy girl. Well, she could certainly put it to better use than we could.

Amira was getting tired by this time, so I picked her up and we all set off along the track towards the large white building in the distance.

'So this bit in the middle must be no-man's land. We could be spies. This is how they do it in films,' I thought.

I didn't look back once. Only forward. It was only a few

hundred yards to walk, but they were the most meaningful steps I had ever taken.

Amira was as heavy as lead in my arms and began struggling to get down. We stopped and she wriggled free. I prized the top off one of the Cokes to give her a drink and she sat down, fighting me for sole rights to the bottle. At this stage I couldn't deal with her spilling it all over her dress, so I opted for the paddy that ensued. It was Leila who ended up drinking the Coke.

My stubborn, independent two-year-old then decided to plant herself firmly in the middle of no-man's land and refused to move.

'Bismileilrahmeilraheem.' Automatically, I gave thanks to God as Mona relieved me of the black bag and carrier with water and fruit inside. She had a smart, silver suitcase on wheels, with a handle that pulled out, and she laid my things on top. Leila carried the Coke, and I wrestled with my thoroughly unco-operative toddler.

Thus we reached the end of the track with the barbed wire. Mona pointed to our bus and we started delightedly towards it, but weren't allowed to get straight on. We had to go through the correct procedure. It was frustrating, but I wasn't unduly worried. Filled with the flush of success after managing to get out of Egypt, I approached the white building ahead of us with new-found confidence.

Entering the building was like being in a different world. The contrast between the two ends of the barbed-wire fence hit me immediately. Gone were the flaky, paint-peeling, stained walls, patched-up furniture and noisy fans. No one was sitting around on the floor, and there were no beggars outside. Instead, the stone floor was spotless, free of cigarette butts and chewing gum. The air-conditioning hummed efficiently. The walls were painted and clean. The whole place smelt of order and civilisation.

I breathed in deeply, inhaling the smell of cleanliness. I had almost forgotten what order and civilisation were. This was me. This was my culture. This was what I wanted for my daughters.

I reached up, removed my headscarf, and pulled out the grips holding my bun in place. My blonde hair fell down in a ponytail, instantly relieving me of my Egyptian image.

'Now I can just be a mum with her children. No more Arabic,' I grinned to myself.

There were seats along one side and little open booths where you could fill in entry forms. This was another shock. I hadn't realised that we would have to fill in a form in order to gain entry to Israel. I had concentrated all my energies into escaping out of Egypt, and had not anticipated any further confrontations.

'No worries, it's just the Israelis demonstrating their efficiency. I don't have a problem with that,' I thought, reaching for one of the pens provided.

A form had to be filled in for everyone entering Israel, including children. When I reached the section headed 'Place and Country of Birth', I paused. Leila had been born in

England, but I had given birth to Amira in Egypt. This could cause a few problems. But how would anyone possibly find out if I lied? After all, she was now on my passport.

I hurriedly made my decision and wrote 'England' in the appropriate box for all three of us. For some unknown reason, that unsure, apprehensive, slightly scared feeling came over me again. Would they find out I had lied? And what would happen to us if they did?

No longer relieved and relaxed, I gathered up the entry forms and stood in the queue to hand them in. It was fairly fast-moving, and I could see that Mona was at the head of the queue. She turned and waved to us, her passport in her hand, indicating that she would wait for us on the bus. I nodded back with a smile, feeling a little better.

We reached the desk, handed in our entry forms and the passport. But instead of waving us through, the man took the time to open the passport and leaf through it. He came to the page where the residency visas for Egypt were stamped and cast his eyes slowly down to the sentence beneath, written in Arabic. This stated that I was the wife of an Egyptian national.

In that moment, I sensed that our problems were nowhere near over. There was a terrible silence as he pondered and we waited. Both girls were standing quietly at my side. It was as if the whole world had stood still. He suddenly closed the passport and set it down on the desk with a bang. Instantly I was alert, waiting to see what would happen.

The man spoke into a telephone briefly and returned his

gaze to me. He was not smiling. I looked down at the children to try and ease the tension.

As he lifted his gaze to look beyond me, I felt a strong hand on my shoulder. I turned and panic suddenly surged through me. The hand belonged to a soldier, and his other hand nursed a huge bayonet.

'This way, madam.'

We followed him into a small side room. There was a desk with two chairs behind it.

'Sit,' he commanded.

As he stood to attention at the door, two more senior officers joined us. I was surprised to see that one of them was female. They had on identical green uniforms. The man held my passport.

'Your luggage. Please to show me your luggage,' he bellowed.

The soldier at the door was instantly at my side, setting the black bag and the two plastic carriers on the table for inspection. The female officer examined the contents of the plastic bags. She spoke in an authoritative tone to him, in English.

'Remove this, all of it.'

'Excuse me, what is happening?'

'We do not allow food or drink into our country like this. You should have deposited it all in the entrance. There is a sign.'

'Sign? I didn't see anything written about food or drink and it is all we have. At least can I keep the bottle of water that has not been opened?' I pleaded. 'My daughters get thirsty very quickly.'

The woman inclined her head very slightly. The young soldier took out the full bottle of water, set it on the desk and departed with the rest of our supplies.

The other officer now leaned forward, his hands linked together in front of him, tapping his thumbs together. His eyes locked onto mine and began to question me in perfect, accent-free English.

'Is this your luggage?'

'Yes, sir.'

'Do you have any other bags?'

'No, sir.'

'Did you pack this bag yourself?'

'Yes, sir.'

'Has anyone had the opportunity to put anything in this bag?'

'No, sir.'

'Has the bag been in your possession at all times?'

'Yes, sir.'

He paused for a moment, his eyes leaving my face to rest for a moment on my black bag. I continued to look directly at him, focusing on his chin and avoiding his eyes. Somehow, if I had looked down, it would have made me appear guilty of something, and I could feel the female officer staring right at me. I had been very careful to address him as 'sir' after every question. This demonstrated subservience and respect, and was something every Moslem woman would do automatically.

The stern manner of questioning brought with it the chilling realisation that they thought I could be a spy or a smuggler of some sort. Relations between the two countries were very tenuous indeed and I was attempting to gain entry without an escort. Maybe they thought the children were a decoy to cover up something far more sinister. From tourist to terrorist in minutes. The gravity of the situation was crystal-clear.

'Why do you have only one small bag? What are your plans during your stay in Israel?'

The questioning resumed, the eyes once again focussed on mine.

'We are travelling only for a short weekend break to see my parents, sir. These are the only things we require for that time.'

'Why do your parents not travel to Egypt to see you?'

'They have been twice to visit us, sir. They have always wanted to visit Israel, and decided to spend two weeks here, hoping that I could join them for a couple of days before returning to work.'

There was a knock on the door. Two young soldiers approached the desk, unzipped the black bag and began to rifle through the contents, spilling them out before us: terry nappies, vests, T-shirts, underwear, dresses, a sponge bag, a pair of my shoes, jackets and a camera. They pounced immediately on the camera, opened the back and ripped out the film.

I was shocked and becoming confused. The force with which they had silently attacked the camera was frightening.

The camera was flung to one side. My shoes were the next objects to be examined. They ripped off one of the heels, then tossed them away.

Then came the sponge bag. Toothpaste was squeezed out of the tube, the hairbrush was taken apart and examined.

Most of the clothes were left undisturbed, until they reached the pile of nappies. There were fifteen. They were obviously at a complete loss. Holding the white square of towelling high up in the air, one of them asked, 'Is this a towel?'

There ensued a private conversation between soldiers and officers in a foreign language, Hebrew I supposed. It was obvious, however, that they could not agree. Voices became louder, more urgent, until the female officer put up her hand to stop them, and turned to me.

'Why do you have so little luggage, but you need fifteen towels? What are they made of? What are you hiding in them? You *must* tell the truth, or it will be worse for you.'

Leila suddenly buried her head in my arm and began to cry. She didn't understand what was going on, and I could give her no reassurances.

'Oh God, they think there's something in the nappies. What? Heroin? Microchips? I'm out of my depth here. What on earth am I going to say?' I cuddled Leila to me as I desperately considered my response. In the end, I did what I considered to be the clearest, most understandable thing.

I lifted Amira up from the floor, pulled up her little dress, and pointed to the nappy she was wearing beneath it.

'They are for my daughter. They are not towels. They are her nappies.'

'Remove this one.'

The officer pointed to Amira's nappy. I realised that he did not believe me, so wearily I went through the process of changing Amira there and then. Of course she was wet and there was a strong smell of urine in the small, clean room. I had to request water, a bag for the wet nappy, talcum powder from the sponge bag and a clean nappy from the desk. By the time I had finished, they believed me. If the situation hadn't been so tragic, it would have been funny. The female officer disposed of the wet nappy and pointed to the pile of clean ones.

'These are for her? But why do you not use Pampers?'

This was such a civilised, yet ignorant question.

'So they have Pampers in Israel,' I thought.

I was unable to tell her the truth, that we could never afford disposable nappies. I was supposed to be well off, able to afford trips to see my parents.

'They are very popular in England,' I finally explained. 'They are much softer on a child's bottom.' I was struggling to provide a believable answer.

At my response, she picked one up and felt it.

'I may take one of these?'

I couldn't believe what I was hearing. There I was, surrounded by military officers who had ransacked my bag and destroyed my few pitiful possessions, and the young woman wanted to take one of my precious nappies.

'Yes, of course, please, take one.' I looked up at her and nodded assent.

One of the soldiers suddenly bent down and picked up Amira's doll from the floor. She screamed as he ripped off the head, without any concern for my little girl. Poor Amira's cries echoed round the room, blocking out anything else, rendering further questioning impossible.

'She's tired and hungry. Could you possibly find something for her to eat?' I shouted over the din.

Having examined the doll and found nothing, the soldier flung it into the bin, stuffed everything back into my bag and zipped it up. He then picked up my screaming daughter and left the room.

'Hey!' I screamed out and started after him, but was immediately restrained by the female officer.

'Please don't worry. He is instructed to take care of her and give her something to eat.'

To my horror, Leila piped up, 'Can I go too, Mama? I'm starving.'

'Of course, you go with this man,' the female officer answered for me and Leila was escorted out as well.

'Now we continue.' It was the voice of the male officer.

'Your daughter spoke in Arabic. Why does she not speak English to you?'

'She is used to Arabic, sir. Most of her friends are Egyptian, as are our family and neighbours there.'

'But she can speak English, yes?'

'Oh yes, sir,' I lied.

'You say you are only staying for a few days. Where do you work?'

'I teach in an English school, sir. I need to be back for Sunday.'

'How will you be travelling back?'

I blessed Jill for her brainwave, and produced the return bus tickets, previously purchased by her on my behalf.

'These are our bus tickets for the return journey, sir.'

I handed them over to him for examination. Satisfied, he relaxed his tone somewhat, and sat back in his chair.

'Where are you intending to meet your parents?'

'In Tel Aviv, sir. They are going to visit Jerusalem next week, but are starting their tour of Israel at Tel Aviv.'

'That will be all.'

Abruptly, he hoisted himself out of the chair and left.

'Stay here,' the female officer ordered, and followed him out of the room.

'My children?' I called after her.

She turned towards me. 'They are safe,' she said, and left, closing the door behind her.

I was alone, my head spinning. What was going on? I had lost control of the situation a long way back, and didn't have a clue how to regain it.

4

Panic and Doubt

Half an hour passed.

The door opened quietly, and two men entered, dressed in civilian clothes. One of them had on a chunky, polo-necked jumper, light grey with flecks of blue in it. There were no guns to be seen.

I jumped up and shouted at them.

'Where are my daughters?' I demanded. I couldn't help myself, I just blurted it out.

'Your daughters are being well taken care of. Please don't worry. You will be able to see them soon. You would like some tea?'

I would have killed for some tea. My throat was parched. The last drink I'd had was in Egypt at the border, after which I had been sick. But more important than tea was to get through these questions and see the girls again.

'No, thank you,' I said.

But then the door opened again, and a large tray with tea, milk, sugar and an ashtray was placed on the desk. The second man poured out a cup for each of us and offered me the milk.

I said nothing. I was tired. I added milk and watched the liquid change colour as I stirred it.

'Cigarette, madam?'

I shook my head as they both lit up, blowing the smoke up to the ceiling. The tea trickled down my throat, giving it new life. There was silence as they smoked and I recharged my batteries by drinking the tea. I could feel my body relaxing.

'We would like to ask you a few questions.'

The man in the jumper spoke quietly and politely, nodding all the while in a reassuring way. He pointed to the black bag.

'Is this your luggage?'

I looked puzzled. 'I have already told the other man that it is.'

'Do you have any other bags?'

'But I have already answered this question,' I began to protest.

'Please, madam. Just answer the questions. Did you pack this bag yourself?'

'Yes, sir.'

Their questions mirrored the previous set exactly. And suddenly I thought I knew why. The first interrogators had been the hard ones and now I was being subjected to the soft touch to see if I would give different answers or 'slip up'. I was slowly regaining some confidence. I would have to be very careful to duplicate my answers exactly. I sat up and concentrated hard on the answers I gave until they had finished their questioning.

'Thank you. Remain here, please.'

They stood up and left. I had no time to think anything through as the original male officer strode back in.

'We wish you a pleasant stay in our country with your parents. Your children are waiting outside. You may now leave.'

He held out my passport. As I took it gratefully from him, I knew that he believed my story. In Egypt, the official at the exit border had seen through me, yet let me through for a decent tip. Here in Israel, it was not only the walls that were painted and clean. These officials were serious about their responsibilities and they had made it their duty to interrogate me until they were absolutely sure I was telling the truth.

The girls were relaxed and only mildly happy to see me. Sitting on the seats that lined the main hall, swinging her little legs to and fro, Amira had chocolate all over her face and they were each sucking on an ice-lolly.

I had not dared to think about the girls' safety when they had been taken from me in that little room. I had been unable to do anything, but I had to trust the officials, even though they could have done anything. I might never have seen my daughters again. Instead of facing my fears, I had concentrated on getting over the interrogation.

Now, seeing them alive, safe and smiling, relief rushed over me and tears streamed down my cheeks. I brushed them quickly away and put on a beaming smile.

'Come on, you two. What took you so long? I've been waiting ages. We've a bus to catch.'

Laughing and giggling together, the doll temporarily for-gotten, we left that huge, white entrance building and walked out into the sunlight to where the bus was still waiting for us.

There were long faces and annoyed comments from the other passengers as we mounted the bus. Understandably, they did not take kindly to a two-hour delay in the middle of their journey. Mona was immediately at our side, genuinely concerned.

'What happened to you? Was there a problem?'

'They asked a lot of questions. It's because I am travelling alone with the children, I suppose.'

A thought suddenly struck me as the bus moved off. 'Mona, why didn't they question you? You are a female travelling alone.'

She smiled. 'That's because I am an Israeli with an Israeli passport, entering my mother country.'

I realised I knew nothing about her. She had asked all the questions. I had assumed she was Egyptian and just tried to get rid of her.

'But when we first met you spoke Arabic fluently.'

Mona laughed. 'I speak four languages fluently, or do you think my English is not good enough?'

'No, of course not. Your English is excellent. I'm sorry I haven't been friendlier towards you. You've been so kind to us all.'

We chatted amiably for the next half-hour, me still being careful to give nothing of importance away. The landscape of Israel was again in stark contrast to the bare desert of Egypt. Everything was suddenly green: fields, trees, bushes with bright-coloured flowers. The roads were built to a high standard, with flyovers and modern bridges. On the outskirts of Jerusalem, the streets were lined with neat, white houses with pretty flowers filling window boxes, creating a mass of colour. It was a welcome relief from the crumbling, grey blocks of flats I had been used to looking at day after day in Cairo.

'This is the richer area of Jerusalem,' explained Mona. 'The inside of the city is more traditional, with old buildings, donkeys and carts, market stalls and women in black. You will see.'

She was right. It was a beautiful, magical place, even through the window of the coach. We drove right through the centre of the city, and out the other side to the bus station.

Mona leaned over and hugged me briefly. 'My stop. My home is in Jerusalem. If you ever want to visit with your lovely daughters, you know you are very welcome. This is my address.'

She held out a little white card, on which her name and address were printed.

'Thanks for everything, Mona. We won't forget you.'

We watched her step down from the coach and waved to her through the window. It had been a chance meeting, but a very fortuitous one.

During the journey from Jerusalem to Tel Aviv I was so emotionally exhausted that I fell into a deep sleep, until suddenly Leila was shaking me awake. We had arrived.

This time I didn't jump for joy or congratulate ourselves for making it. I had learned from the events of today not to assume anything, and I was still very wary. I was scanning the area for soldiers, guns or any uniforms.

'Let everyone else get off first. We don't want to be squashed.'

I watched the other passengers get off and go to the side of the coach to collect their luggage. There was a line of taxis to one side. Some of the passengers went towards them, others wandered out into the street. There was no sign of any officials at all.

'Okay girls, let's go.'

We made our way along the aisle and down the steps. Outside, I led the way to a waiting taxi. The driver jumped out.

'*Shalom.*'

'*Shalom,*' I replied, hoping that this was the correct thing to say.

'*Shalom, shalom, shalom,*' sang Amira.

'Well, that takes the biscuit,' I thought. 'Her Arabic is developing well, but not her English. I take her out of the country, and she greets the first man we meet in his language.'

'We would like to go to this hotel, please.'

I held out the piece of paper with the name written on it.

He nodded. 'Airport.'

'Excuse me?'

'Hotel. Airport. I take you to hotel. No problem.'

Fifteen minutes into the journey, the driver pointed out of the window. 'Airport. Look. Here airport.'

I nodded and smiled. This was why the hotel had been chosen. It was the closest to the airport.

The journey took about twenty minutes and cost $9. I gave him $10 and we went up the hotel steps and into the reception.

'*Shalom.*'

'*Shalom.* A double room just for the night, please.'

'Yes, of course, madam. Could you sign here?'

I signed the book and she handed me a key.

'Do you have any luggage?'

I froze and looked around. But no one was waiting to question me. I looked at the receptionist and saw that she was smiling. For a moment I had been back in the interrogation room.

'No, just this one bag. I can manage, thank you. I would like to pay now please, as we are leaving for the airport early in the morning.'

'That will be $32.'

'I would like an alarm call for five-thirty tomorrow morning and a taxi at six to take us to the airport,' I added, handing over the money.

'Yes, madam, no problem.'

A porter showed us up the two flights of stairs, took the key from me and opened the door. The room was in darkness. He walked across to the heavy curtains and opened them. Early evening sunlight filtered through, lighting up the whole room. He bowed politely and left. I didn't tip him, although it was obviously the thing to do. I wasn't sure how much money I would need and couldn't risk spending any of it unnecessarily.

I dumped the bag on the floor and flung myself, with a whoop of joy, onto the bed, burying my face in the pillows. I bounced back up, caught Amira as she was toddling round the bed, and swung her round and round until we collapsed giggling in a dizzy heap.

It wasn't likely that anyone had followed us here. For the next few hours at least, we could relax. We explored the room, Leila opening every drawer and cupboard. It was all so luxurious to us. By the main door was a second door, which led to a spacious ensuite bathroom with a bath.

'Look out there, Mama. Is it a swimming pool? Can we go swimming?'

Leila had ventured out onto the balcony and was looking down into the hotel grounds.

'Let's go and see, shall we?'

We all went out to explore. It was six o'clock. A mere thirteen hours previously, I had been looking down on my husband with his self-satisfying smile, as he slept in our lumpy bed in Egypt. So much had happened since then.

'Has he realised we have gone? What will he be doing now?' I wondered. 'He won't even consider that we have left the country, as he has my passport firmly under lock and key. It would never enter his head that I could have another one processed by the British Embassy. With all the people he tips to tell him my every movement, he won't even dream that I would be capable of such a thing. That will give us more time. If we do succeed and get away, it will be a few days before that possibility even occurs to him. He'll waste time searching at the school and at friends' houses, thinking that we're hiding somewhere in Egypt.'

We walked around to where Leila had seen the huge, sand-blasted wall with the chrome steps at the top. Yes, she was right, it was indeed a swimming pool, but when we looked over the wall, there wasn't any water in it.

'Never mind. I know what we can do. How about going back to the room for a hot bath? That's just as good as swimming in a pool, isn't it?'

'Yes, let's go.' Leila took the room key from me and skipped ahead, singing as she went.

Amira joined in, '*Shalom, shalom, shalom,*' and tried to keep up.

That should tire them both out, I thought. I daren't buy anything else. I really needed to save the few dollars I had left. We'd just have to go without any tea that night and exist on the bottle of water. I was used to going without food, but the girls weren't.

I reached the room and had to knock for Leila to let me in.

'Look, Mama.' She danced around the room with nothing but a towel wrapped around her. The towels were clean and soft.

'Where's Amira?'

'In the bathroom. I couldn't turn the taps on the bath. They were too stiff.'

She led the way to the bathroom, but the door had closed and it had locked itself. We turned the knob, pushed and pulled, but the door did not budge.

'Oh God, this is just what we need! Amira!' I shouted. 'Amira, darling. Can you hear me? Have you locked the door from the inside?'

But Amira just banged on the door from her side. I knew there was little point in asking her to try and unlock it.

'Amira, don't touch the taps. Mama will get someone to open the door.'

I rushed to the phone and rang down to reception. The same porter came immediately with a key. Within minutes the problem had been resolved, without panic or distress.

This time, I couldn't let the porter leave without a tip. I gave him $2, for which he seemed very grateful.

We had a great time in that bathroom, using the bubble bath provided. Amira was not at all impressed with having nothing but water for tea. There were tears, and she eventually fell asleep on the bed, exhausted.

'When can we see Nanna?'

Leila and I sat out on the balcony. It was time to tell her the truth.

'Leila, if I were to tell you that Nanna and Grandad are not coming to Israel on holiday, but we are going to see them in England instead, would you mind?'

I held my breath, waiting for her answer.

Of course, she answered with another question. 'For always, Mama?'

Her immediate acceptance of the changing situation was totally unexpected. No questions about holidays in Israel, why we ever came to the country in the first place or why Nanna wasn't coming. Her desire to escape from her life in Cairo forever and begin a new one with her Nanna was all that mattered to her. It struck a powerful chord within me, at the same time giving me all the reassurance I needed that I had made the right choice in risking everything to get out.

'Yes, darling. Forever and ever.'

5

Catastrophe

With both girls asleep, I had another important task ahead of me. Quietly, I lifted the receiver and made a reverse charges call to my parents in England.

'Hello?'

'Dad? It's me. We've made it. I'm calling from the hotel you picked out for me in Tel Aviv.'

Silence.

'Dad? Are you there?'

Mum's voice came on the line.

'Yes, he's here. He just can't speak at the moment. It's all a bit too much for him.' Her voice broke and she began to cry.

'Oh Jacky, you've no idea. We've been willing you to make it, every step of the way. Are the girls all right?'

'Fine. We're all fine. Our plane lands at Heathrow tomorrow morning at twenty past eleven.'

'We'll be there, my darling. Oh Jacky, I can't believe it. You've actually done it. You're so brave.'

'See you both in the morning then. I love you.'

* * *

As the tears rolled down my cheeks, I stood under the hot shower and let the stress and strain of the day wash away. This morning I had been a Moslem wife and mother, this afternoon, an English mother in Israel. Tomorrow morning I would be a single parent in England.

I sat on a chair and counted out the remaining money. It didn't take long: $16. How had I managed to spend so much? The taxi, the room and the porter totalled $44, I realised. As far as I knew, the only thing we would need to pay for was the taxi to the airport, a short, five-minute journey. So $16 should be ample.

I smiled to myself. Despite everything, we had made it this far, and all we had to do now was to get on that plane to London. I slipped into the bed, snuggled up beside the girls and closed my eyes.

'I won't sleep, I'm far too excited,' I thought. I turned over, and sat up in alarm as the room telephone rang out. Cautiously, I picked up the receiver.

'Yes?' I whispered.

'Good morning, madam. This is your five-thirty wake-up call.'

Astounded, I replaced the receiver and went to look out of the window. It was certainly morning. I must have slept after all.

The telephone had woken us all. Leila switched on the TV and she and Amira sat, goggle-eyed, in front of it as I struggled to do their hair with the broken hairbrush. There was even time for a quick bath for Amira to freshen her up, before leaving that wonderful hotel.

The taxi was waiting. There was not a lot of traffic on the roads and within ten minutes we were standing outside the airport building. The taxi fare amounted to $4.

'Can we get something to eat?'

'We must wait until we get on the plane, Leila. There'll be plenty to eat then. Right now I need to find the office to collect our tickets.'

'Will it take long?'

'I should say about half an hour, that's all. But without the tickets, we can't get on the plane at all.'

I scanned the airport. There were people milling around, but it was not crowded. Despite this, I still couldn't locate the ticket office, so we approached a woman at one of the check-in desks, who directed us up a small flight of stairs.

At the top, there was a long corridor with an office immediately to our right. It was tiny but airy, with large windows on two sides, through which I could see three people working.

I knocked on the open door and waited.

'Good morning,' I offered.

'Good morning. How can I help?' replied one of the girls, standing up with a smile. Her English accent was very good.

I smiled back at her.

'Our tickets for this morning's flight to London Heathrow have been telexed to us. I would like to collect them, please.'

'Of course. One moment, please. Your passport?'

I handed it over and she disappeared, returning within minutes followed by a tall, thin man with a moustache.

'This way, madam, if you please.'

We all trailed after him down a corridor into another room. It was square and sparse, with only a table and chairs dotted around.

'Please wait here. We are trying to find the tickets.'

I smiled and nodded.

'They are very considerate,' I thought. 'Giving us a cool room to sit down in. There was nowhere to sit in that tiny office.'

Two men entered. One had my passport in his hand. He indicated to a chair at the table.

'Please sit here, madam.'

The other man held a large bag of sunflower seeds, *lib*, which he was shelling with his teeth in the traditional way. As I stood to change seats, he went to sit with the children.

The first man sat at the table opposite me and opened my passport.

'You are the wife of an Egyptian.'

It was a statement, rather than a question. I kept quiet.

'You entered our country only yesterday. You stay at a hotel out of the city, yet convenient for the airport. Now you are requesting tickets for London.'

He paused.

'He's guessed. He's not going to let us have the tickets. He's going to send us back.' My mind was racing.

'Why did you come to Israel for only a few hours?'

'We intended staying for three days, sir, to meet with my parents, but then our circumstances changed.'

It was as if he had not heard me speak. He continued,

42

'Whom have you spoken to? Have you met anyone or made any phone calls?'

'I have spoken only to the hotel staff. I have made one international call to England, sir.'

'Do you speak Hebrew?'

'No, sir.'

'To whom did you make the call?'

'To my mother, sir.'

'But your parents are in Israel, no?'

'No, sir. They were coming for a holiday, and we have travelled here today in order to meet them. But there is a problem. My father has suffered a heart attack and is now in hospital. It is for this reason that he has telexed air tickets for us to fly to England to see him.'

I crossed my fingers on both hands as I looked innocently back at him.

'Where is your luggage?'

'This is the only bag I have, sir. I was not expecting to fly to England. This was all we needed for a few days in Israel'.

'Open the bag.'

As I unzipped the black holdall allowing him to rifle through its contents, I thought how fortunate that we had not brought any more. This solitary bag supported my story well and made it all the more believable.

'So your father is ill. You must go to him, of course. I hope he recovers quickly.' He stood up, handed back the bag and turned to leave. 'Your passport, madam. The tickets are in the next office. I will have them brought to you directly. Have an enjoyable trip.'

'Thank you, sir.'

The other man stood up with the girls. They had been sharing the sunflower seeds from his bag, but now he bent down and filled each of their hands with them. They were delighted and immediately began shelling them for themselves.

We collected the tickets from the next office and made our way back down into the main hall of the airport building.

'Over there, Leila. To the baggage check. We're almost there now.'

The bag trundled through the X-ray machine without any flashing lights or alarm bells. I collected it at the other side, and prepared to enter the boarding lounge.

'We've done it. All those questions and they still let us through. There can be no more questions now. We are safe.'

Relief surged through me. The plane was so close. Soon we would be sitting on it. The boarding lounge loomed closer. I began to smile.

An official standing to one side suddenly stepped out in front of us and laid his hand on my shoulder.

Startled, I cried out and shied away. What on earth could he want?

'Excuse me, madam. You need to pay the airport tax. Over here, please.'

I realised then that I should have gone to pay this before the baggage check.

'Oh yes. Of course.'

We walked to the desk. I handed over the tickets and my passport.

'That will be $16, please.'

I shook my head in disbelief.

'How much did you say?'

'$16.'

A single tear ran down my cheek and dripped onto the desk. I could feel Leila's little hand tighten in my own. I'd risked our lives, survived all the questions, managed to keep the girls happy, and Mum and Dad would be in London by now to meet us. This was the final hurdle. I looked up at the man.

'I'm sorry. I don't have enough.'

'If you cannot pay', he said, 'you cannot board the plane to London.'

I covered my face with both hands. I had to decide what to do now and where to go. Only two things were certain in my mind. One was that we could never return to Egypt. As for the other, well, it was about everything we had been through during the last twenty-four hours.

It had all been for nothing.

6

The Beginning

'Good morning, ladies and gentlemen. This is your captain speaking. We are now approaching Cairo airport, and will land in approximately ten minutes. The time is 6.50 a.m. local time. I hope you have enjoyed the flight and thank you for flying with KLM.'

The heat smacked into me as I stepped off the plane, and I wondered what on earth could be causing it. As I looked around, I realised that this was the normal weather at 7 a.m. in Cairo. Waves of hot air swirled in front of me, making the airport building and the figures hurrying this way and that appear wobbly, not quite in focus. It was such a total contrast to the dark, wet, bitterly cold and blustery November evening we had left behind in London only a few hours earlier.

I was so excited. This was completely different, what I'd dreamed about. The holiday of a lifetime. Ahead of me stretched ten wonderful days exploring this beautiful, hot, sandy country.

Dave wasn't so keen, but then again, he had the passionate, excitable, impressionable side of his nature firmly under wraps. His feet were firmly on the ground. He knew what he wanted, and at the moment he was embarking on a short holiday to Egypt for a break in his routine, an opportunity to do nothing, relax and get totally drunk wherever and whenever he could.

The first opportunity to achieve this objective had already arrived on the plane and he was well on the road to being a happy and satisfied human being. I doubt if he had any first impressions of this ancient land that he would be able to recall today.

I was part of what he wanted. I was twenty-three and we had been together for about three years. There was nothing particularly wrong with our relationship, except that the spark had disappeared. We had originally booked this holiday six months ago in the hope of bringing it to life again. Since then, however, things had gone from bad to worse.

Our relationship had been under increasing strain as our lives branched out in different directions, and at different times of the day. I had a nine-to-five job working in an office for Kodak, surrounded by colleagues, constantly meeting new people. Dave had followed me from the north to the south of England and found a job as a milkman, hauling himself out of bed at four o'clock every morning. For him it was a lonely working day unless he was collecting money from his round.

Slowly our lives began to separate until it was no longer possible to ignore the fact. To confront what was happening to us would mean confronting our feelings and facing up to the fact that we no longer wanted the same things. So we did what most people do, when what they actually need to do is communicate. We booked a holiday, return flights, ten days, London – Cairo – London. Make or break time.

But with the departure date looming, I had known in my heart that it was break time. How on earth would I be able to tell him?

'After the holiday,' I told myself. 'We'll sort things out then.'

And so they were. Things. Sorted out. But not in my wildest dreams could I have imagined how.

7

Why Bus Fares Are So Cheap

The noise was coming at us from all directions. There were people everywhere, women in black from head to foot, other women wearing the veil, girls with scarves around their heads and faces, babies crying, men in *galabeyas*. Everyone was shouting, calling out and gesticulating wildly. No one was answering.

'Taxi, taxi, madam?'

'You buy zees – very nice, very cheap, no many dollars.'

The traders hassled everyone. Young girls were begging, or mothers with children sat on the ground, barefoot, hands outstretched, calling out, '*Baksheesh, baksheesh.*'

Some of the children had dreadful deformities, bent legs or club-feet, which they displayed for us to see. Naturally our instinct was to take pity on them and open our purses. Traders and beggars alike, they were excellent at their job, as tourists dug deep into their pockets for money to oblige.

'What shall we do, then?'

Dave dropped his rucksack onto the ground as he looked around.

'Taxi or bus? Taxis are right over the other side. The bus

stop is just up here.'

I walked up to the stop. We had strayed beyond the taxi rank directly outside the airport to avoid the beggars.

'I think a bus would be much more authentic. There's one coming now.'

'Right you are, then.'

Dave picked up his rucksack and joined me.

This proved to be our first big mistake. Foreigners just did not attempt to catch a bus.

A battered, ancient, single-decker bus screeched to a halt. It was empty. Dave boarded first.

'Cairo city centre?'

The driver smiled broadly, revealing horrible, brown, broken teeth with as many gaps. He began to babble in a strange language: '*El Kohera, El Kohera.*'

He beckoned us on board, nodding and smiling.

Dave looked unsure. 'What's he on about? What's this *Kohaira?*'

'How do I know? Cairo maybe? Show him some money, see how much it is,' I suggested.

Dave took out some Egyptian pound notes and offered them to the driver. He took one pound and handed back change, sixty piastres. Just twenty piastres, a few pence each for a ride into the city. Amazing. We were about to find out why.

During the next ten minutes, all the jokes about how many elephants you can squeeze into a telephone box sprung to mind, as what appeared to be the total population of Africa piled on to this bus. The seats were gradually filled, women squashing children, babies and shopping onto the seat with them. One woman, swathed in black, had a large basket containing about six chickens on her head. She perched it on the back of a seat. People were standing and squatting everywhere.

'Surely there is no more room,' Dave whispered to me. 'Oh my God, look!'

Men and young boys were hoisting themselves onto the roof. Others were standing on the bumpers and hanging on to each other. I couldn't see how the bus was ever going to move at all.

But move it did. The engine spluttered into life and with a belch of exhaust fumes, the bus lurched along. Through a tiny patch of window, I could make out another identical bus groaning to a halt. Men, women, children and chickens were all over it, shouting and clucking hysterically as they got out.

I dug Dave in the ribs. 'That must be what we look like. Can you believe it?'

'At least their journey's over. What are our chances of survival, do you think?'

I smiled. 'I'll let you know.'

It was dreadfully hot and difficult to breathe. The bus was travelling fast, swerving round corners, jolting over the uneven roads. Dave stood up and let an old woman sit in his seat. Her face was covered in wrinkles, her wrists covered with gold bangles. Swathed in black, she extended a bony arm to grasp the seat in front to maintain her balance and I noticed a pale blue tattoo just above the bangles.

Two children peered round at me, staring at my blonde hair and giggling. Then one of them leaned over and tried to touch me. They kept repeating something. The language was guttural and they spoke very fast. I had no idea what they meant. I turned my head to a patch of window and watched the landscape change from villages and cows to buildings, high walls, mosques and minarets.

'Jacky, come on, let's get off here. I'll forge a way. Come on.' Dave was literally pushing and shoving his way to the exit.

'Okay.'

Hurriedly I stood up, preparing myself for the battle ahead. I squeezed past the old woman, but then I just couldn't manage to move at all.

The noise of the passengers suddenly reached a crescendo as one of the baskets overturned and two chickens escaped. I tried desperately to keep an eye firmly on Dave, but a great panic erupted as everyone tried to recapture the hysterical chickens. Women were screaming at the tops of their voices, men were diving on top of each other and the chickens were flapping madly up and down the bus. There was a sea of dust and feathers, causing people to cough and splutter, and then wipe their noses on their sleeves or robes. One woman screamed as a chicken scrabbled frantically over her head, dragging her veil with it and revealing her dark, lustrous hair. I recoiled as hands reached out from all directions to touch me.

'Dave, help me,' I shouted as loudly as I could.

The bus swerved to a stop and everyone standing fell on top of one another. I managed to stand up, but could no longer see Dave. Clinging on to my backpack and handbag for dear life, fighting back tears, I ended up being pushed down the bus instead of up, as it moved off again, quickly gathering speed, lurching and swerving.

Amid the throng of bodies, I pushed forward. As the bus groaned to another halt, I reached the back exit and managed the first step down. The bus started to move off again. I knew I'd never be able to hang on, so I closed my eyes – and jumped.

Dave was not there. He did not step out of the shade, arms outstretched to catch me. He wasn't even standing nearby. He was nowhere to be seen.

I had landed in a heap in the gutter, covered in dust from the belching fumes of the departing bus. The sun was beating down, my mouth was dry and dusty, sweat was trickling down my face and had seeped through my blouse. I felt relieved to have left the bus, yet suddenly terrified about the situation I now found myself in.

I looked around for Dave. He had to be somewhere. He must have got off at the previous stop. He would now be in hot pursuit to find me, I was sure. I shaded my eyes and stared intently up and down the wide street. He was so easily recognisable with his shoulder-length hair and moustache, his scruffy jeans and T-shirt.

At this point, I was still sitting at the side of the kerb in a heap, where I had landed. 'I'll be able to see better if I stand up,' I decided.

It was only then that I realised something was not quite right. As soon as I tried to put any pressure on my right foot, a searing pain ripped through my ankle. I sat down again to check. It was swelling and aching like mad.

I slipped off my trainer, pushed it into the top of my backpack, hauled myself upright on the other leg and scanned the street once more for Dave. But there was no sign of him, and Dave never came.

8

Tea and Sympathy

As I waited under the hot sun, it slowly dawned on me that I was totally alone. Fear and then panic swiftly replaced sadness.

Looking around, I saw that it was not a bustling, busy street as I had imagined Cairo to be. There were no huge department stores or shops; in fact it appeared to be more residential, with little shops dotted about. There was still a lot of traffic, providing a great deal of noise. People were wandering around. This must be a suburb of Cairo, or on the outskirts, I realised.

A white Peugeot estate car pulled up beside me. Two men jumped out and bent over me, gabbling loudly in Arabic. Their behaviour and gestures were non-threatening, and they made no attempt to touch me in any way. I didn't try to run away. I couldn't have even if I'd wanted to. My ankle was swelling up and throbbing.

'You speak English?'

I looked up and nodded.

'You come here.' He pointed to the pavement in the shade of the buildings. 'Come, no sun here.'

He helped me hobble to the other side of the pavement. The other man brought my rucksack. He then reached up to the green shutters above him and banged heavily on them.

A woman flung open the shutters, shouting angrily down to the man. They proceeded to hold a very loud conversation, him gesticulating towards me all the while. She remained aggressive throughout, yet the man with me nodded and smiled.

'You come, in here. She can help you.'

I looked back up to the shutters, but they had already been closed. This time there was a small gap left between them. I hesitated. She was a formidable woman who certainly looked very hostile. But then these men hadn't planned on meeting me. They could have left me in distress, yet they stopped and offered to help.

By this time, my ankle was throbbing badly. Everything I knew and felt safe with had disappeared. I now felt panic rising at the thought of being deserted. The men were waiting patiently, not hassling me, as I finally made the decision to go into the building with them.

I nodded in assent and between them they supported me up the five or six concrete steps into the building. It was a block of flats. The formidable woman was now at the front door of her flat, on the right-hand side, and she ushered us inside.

The door opened straight into a sitting-room, with upholstered seats around two walls, a coffee table and a rug. A black-and-white television was switched on in the corner, with a fan on top, blowing air around the room. I was helped down onto the seat, with my leg raised out in front of me. I lifted my face up to catch the effect of the rotating fan as it blew the cool air my way. It felt wonderful.

Unsmiling, the woman approached me and inspected my ankle. She took hold of my leg roughly, until I cried out in protest. Ignoring me totally, she barked out orders along a dark hallway leading off the room and dropped my leg back down onto the seat.

Within minutes, a girl of about fifteen appeared with ice wrapped in a rag, which she gently placed on my ankle. Her black hair was tied back to reveal a heart-shaped face with well-defined cheekbones. Tall and slim with glasses perched on her nose, she was an attractive girl. She looked right at me and smiled.

'You are English, no?'

I nodded.

'My name is Salma. I learn English at school. I love to speak English.'

I was both astounded and delighted. As we chatted, it became apparent that her English was not as polished as it had first appeared; nevertheless we were able to make each other understand with gestures and a dictionary. I managed to make her understand that I had come to Egypt with a friend whom I had lost, and that I was anxious to find him.

The two men stood, looking on. They were dressed in normal clothes, jeans and T-shirts. However, Salma and her mother, the aggressive woman, were dressed in long night-dresses, called *galabeyas*, as I learned later.

It transpired that there was a youth hostel not far away. Dave and I had agreed to look for one when we had planned the holiday. This was good news. At least I now had somewhere to start looking for him. I relaxed a little.

Another girl appeared with a glass of lemon juice on a little silver tray. She had a friendly face with a wide, beaming smile and a much fuller figure than Salma. She was also wearing a long nightdress. She offered the tray to me enthusiastically.

I turned to Salma.

'How do I say "Thank you" in Arabic?'

'*Shokran.*'

'*Shokran,*' I repeated carefully, taking the drink.

Her face lit up. She gabbled on and on, using dramatic gestures. I concentrated carefully, trying to grasp at any little thing that would give me the slightest clue as to what she was saying. My puzzled expression didn't bother her. Others in the room began to speak, and a loud conversation in Arabic ensued. For the moment, everyone ignored me.

I sat tight and sipped my drink. Salma suddenly got up and left the room. I was immediately on my guard, feeling vulnerable among so many strangers.

The silence that followed was more menacing than the fracas had ever been. An elderly man, dressed in his pyjamas, entered from the inner hallway, escorted by Salma. He approached me, bent over, took my hand and shook it.

'*Ahlan, ahlan.*'

Tea appeared, black, heavily sugared, in glasses, again on a silver tray. I began to understand that one glass was for him and the other for me. Something told me to accept graciously. Somehow it did not seem appropriate to say that sugar in tea made me want to throw up, and where on earth was the milk?

Everyone looked on quietly as we drank. I took little sips, drinking the tea in order not to appear rude, but I had to muster all my self-control to stop my face contorting each time it touched my lips and trickled down my throat. In fact, I was concentrating so hard that, when I triumphantly set the empty glass down on the tray, there remained only Salma and the man in the room with me.

The old man set his empty glass back on the tray, stood up and shook my hand once more. Pointing to my ankle, he said a few words to Salma and left the room.

'My father says you must stay here with us until your leg is better.'

My ankle had swollen to twice its size. I was grateful, but anxious to go to the youth hostel.

'Thank you. He is very kind. But I need to go to the youth hostel to try and find my friend. Can you tell me how to get there? Is it far?'

'Too far for you to walk. I will ask my brother, Omar, to take you in the car. This is okay?'

I smiled. 'This is very okay.'

She disappeared. I lay back on the seat, closing my eyes. The family, if a little strange, was being very kind to me.

About fifteen minutes later, Salma returned. She had changed out of her nightdress and flip-flops. She was dressed very smartly in a brown skirt, cream blouse and court shoes.

Her hair was piled up neatly on her head and her face carefully made up. Behind her came one of the men who had helped me in the street.

'My brother, Omar.' Salma introduced him formally to me.

As he shook my hand, he held it fractionally longer than I expected. He smiled and looked into my eyes.

'Hello. English no good. Pardon.'

I laughed. 'Better than my Arabic, though.'

His eyes were very attractive, I noticed. 'In fact, you're gorgeous,' I acknowledged to myself, as Salma translated for me.

'We can go now,' she then said.

Together they helped me out of the building into the white Peugeot estate. As I settled myself in the back seat, loud noises or a kind of droning started up all around us. I looked out of the window, but could not see where it was coming from. It dominated all other outside noise.

'Salma, what is that noise?'

I had to cover my ears for her to understand.

'Oh yes, "noise". It is for *deen* (religion). The man calls and we go to speak to Allah.'

'To pray? Is it a call to prayer?'

'Yes, yes,' she replied excitedly. 'You are Christian, yes?'

I nodded.

She continued, 'My family is Moslem. We have Islam and Mohamed and the man calls and we pray.'

From the driver's seat, Omar raised his hand, his fingers stretched out.

'Five,' he stated. 'Five prays.'

'We go to church to pray every Sunday,' I said.

'Yes, and we pray five times every day,' said Salma.

I was amazed. I bent down in the car to stare up to the top of the minaret from where the wailing was booming out. It went on and on.

'I can't see the man, Salma. Where is he?'

'No man there,' she replied. 'There is cassette. We have a man in the big mosque in Cairo. Here in our street there is cassette.'

I smiled, secretly wishing the tape would snap. This was normal to these people. To me it was an awful din.

We set off, arriving at the youth hostel just minutes later. There was a flight of steps leading up to the entrance. Salma went in first to inquire about Dave, but returned almost immediately.

'Not open now,' she said. 'It will open later this afternoon. You stay with us tonight. You sleep with me.'

'Pardon?'

'Omar will return to ask about your friend. You come with us.'

They hardly knew me, but Salma had assumed I would be staying with them.

This would never happen in England, I thought. The hospitality of these foreigners is very tempting. I could write a note for Omar to leave for Dave so that he would know I was okay and I could arrange to meet him the following day. I turned to Salma with a grateful smile.

'Thank you, Salma. Yes, I will stay with you tonight.'

We returned to the flat, and this time I was directed along the dark corridor off which a kitchen, bathroom and three bedrooms all led.

'This one, please.' Salma helped me into the room at the end. The whole family was gathered there, in their *galabeyas*, lying on the two double beds that lined two sides of the room. I saw that the green shutters were the ones that the woman had flung open when I had been sitting in the street outside earlier. A tall fan on a stand was blowing air around the room.

'*Housh*, Mohamed, *housh*.' The woman pushed the man roughly off the bed to accommodate me.

Salma introduced me to the woman, 'Mama', her other two brothers, Mohamed and Tarek, her talkative sister, Magda, and her father, 'Papa'. They were delighted to meet me, and even Mama smiled and laughed with the others. They had fun pronouncing my name, 'Jacky'. They all said the 'J' as a soft 'G', and could not say 'J'. Papa taught me the numbers in Arabic from one to ten. I managed to repeat them one by one, but couldn't remember them without help.

Eventually Mama hustled the men out into another room for their siesta and left Salma with me while she and Magda disappeared into the kitchen to prepare dinner.

'Do you have paper and a pen for me to write to my friend?'

'Here.' Before I could protest, she had ripped a page from her school exercise book.

I wrote quickly, 'Dear Dave, Have sprained my ankle. Met

some kind people who are letting me stay with them tonight. I'll come to the youth hostel tomorrow.'

I paused. 'What time can we go to the hostel tomorrow, Salma?'

'My brothers will take the car in the morning, so it's better that we wait until the afternoon.'

I continued. 'Try to be at the reception for half past five. Take care. See you soon. Jacky.' I folded the paper and slipped it into my pocket.

Salma, now changed back into her *galabeya*, lay on her bed reading *The Thirty-Nine Steps*, in English. I helped her with pronunciation and tried to explain the meaning of some difficult words. The activity turned out to be fun; we laughed a lot, until Mama and Magda came in and lay down together on the other bed for their siesta. It was obvious that Mama wanted quiet; she turned off the fan and the light and closed the shutters completely. Salma and I lay down together on her bed. I closed my eyes, but could still sense the closeness of Salma's body next to mine. I wasn't used to such intimacy, but it obviously didn't bother her at all.

At five o'clock I awoke to the sound of pans clashing. A tomato-ey, garlicky smell wafted through from the kitchen. I was alone in the room.

'Jacky, we will eat now. You are hungry?'

I sat up, rubbing my eyes.

'Yes. I'm starving.'

Salma looked puzzled. 'Jacky, what is this "starving"?'

'Sorry,' I replied, 'I mean I'm very hungry.' I rubbed my stomach and she smiled.

'Good.'

Mohamed and Omar entered, carrying newspapers, which they spread on the floor of the bedroom. Mohamed was the youngest of the three brothers. He was tall with black hair and glasses. He had a more modern look of an American college student, sometimes keeping his jeans and shirt on in the house when the rest of the family changed into *galabeyas*. He was a mild-mannered boy with a soft voice, in contrast to the eldest brother and first-born, Tarek.

Tarek was a tall, overweight man with a thick moustache, which turned down at the sides and matched his frown. His eyes were dark and shifty and his voice was gruff. He came into the room carrying spoons and huge rounds of brown pitta bread, which he placed on the newspaper. Papa entered and took his place, squatting down. Mama, Magda and Salma brought large, steaming saucepans containing rice, vegetables, meat and chicken in a tomato sauce.

Omar came over to me. 'I help,' he stated with a smile.

As he helped me to sit down on the floor by the newspaper, I threw a questioning look at Salma.

'I teach him,' she said proudly.

I looked back at Omar. '*Shokran.*'

He was impressed. I could tell by the way that he looked at me. I held his gaze fractionally, before looking away.

* * *

Everyone was now sitting on the floor, ready to eat. Papa tore a piece from one of the huge rounds of bread and dipped it into a saucepan. As the sauce seeped up from the bottom, he twisted the bread round to catch a piece of meat as well, held it up and dropped it into his mouth.

This was the cue for us all to begin. I looked round for a plate, knife or fork and watched the food being devoured very deftly with bread, fingers and spoons for the rice.

I decided to tuck in and have a go, but still couldn't resist a private joke with myself. 'This way round, it's a great saving on a table and chairs, not to mention the washing-up.'

I was starving. I started with some chicken. It tasted delicious. I looked over at Mama and pointed to the pan of chicken.

'Good, very good.'

A huge beaming smile spread over her face, changing and softening her appearance. She looked almost attractive and certainly less formidable.

'*Hellwa*,' she replied.

'This means "nice", I think.' Salma leaned over to me.

'*Hellwa*,' I repeated. I pointed at Salma. '*Hellwa*.'

They all laughed at this, nodding their heads. Papa was delighted. Things were going well.

I decided to try some rice. Picking up a spoon, I began filling a piece of torn-off bread with it. Conversation, which had been loud and enthusiastic, suddenly stopped. I looked up. Papa was standing up, his fist clenched. He began to shout angrily, waving his hands in the air and flinging his food back into one of the pans.

The rest of the family stood up. They all began shouting at the same time. Mama was very aggressive, pointing at Papa and digging him in the chest. He responded by hitting her across the face with the flat of his hand and leaving the room.

Mama slumped on one of the beds, pulled a cotton hankie from the top of her nightdress and began to weep and wail, making a terrible noise. Magda comforted her. Mohamed and Tarek resumed eating. The crisis, whatever it was, was over.

Omar leant down, gently removed the spoon from my hand and helped me into another room. Salma followed with a dictionary, and tried to explain.

It turned out that I was the cause of the disruption. I had grossly insulted the family's hospitality, and Papa was refusing to eat in the same room as me. I had eaten food with my left hand, which was totally unacceptable to them.

'Always eat with your right hand,' Salma explained. 'The left is for cleaning the bottoms.'

I had no idea what she meant by that. All I knew at this point was, I must never eat with my left hand again.

9

Desire

'Give me the letter, please. My brother will take it to the youth hostel now.'

Salma held out her hand to take the note. As I reached into my pocket, Omar strolled into the room and my heart gave a sudden, involuntary lurch. I blushed as he smiled at me.

He took the note from Salma and left.

'Do you watch *tamsalayas?*' she asked.

We searched in vain for the English in the dictionary.

'Never mind. You come and watch with me. We see this every day,' she enthused.

I readily agreed, curious to see what this activity would turn out to be, and hobbled into the back bedroom. I passed Papa's room on the way, and could hear a television on in there, but the door was closed.

Salma crossed the room and switched on another television. A man and a woman were overacting very dramatically on a very amateur set.

'This is *tamsalaya*. You have this in England?'

'Yes, we have many programmes like this. They are called "soaps".'

Salma burst out laughing. 'Soaps,' she repeated. 'English is so funny.'

She lay on her tummy, resting her chin on her hands, totally engrossed.

The screen glazed over as my mind drifted. I couldn't understand any of the Egyptian soap, although it was clear that the actors were very stilted and wooden. I wondered what Omar was doing and when he would get back. My concern with finding Dave was forgotten.

When Omar returned with the news that Dave had not yet registered at the hostel, and that he had left my note for him, I had mixed emotions. I was concerned for Dave's welfare, but secretly relieved, as it gave me more time to be in the company of such a hospitable and generous family, in spite of Papa's violent outburst.

'I could stay here forever with you,' I thought, 'but this one night will have to do.'

'Someone is here to see you.'

We had been relaxing, watching an Indian film on the television, with Arabic subtitles, when the doorbell rang. Salma had gone to answer the door.

'How on earth has Dave managed to find me here?' I thought. 'Maybe Omar left his address at the hostel.'

As Omar took my arm to help me into the sitting-room to receive the visitor, all thoughts of Dave vanished. I was conscious of the closeness of his body and the touch of his strong arm that was supporting me.

There was no one in the sitting-room. I sat down with my leg raised. Angry voices were coming from Papa's room. There was the sound of someone approaching. I looked up, wondering what I was going to say.

But instead of Dave, a small, attractive woman, her head covered in a white veil, strode into the room and shook my hand firmly.

'Hallo. I am *Tante* Fatma. I am sister of Ibrahim.'

She bent down and kissed me on both cheeks, and grasped my cheeks with one hand and squeezed them gently, before releasing them.

'*Assal, assal.*'

'Ibrahim is Papa's name. Aunt Fatma say you are like honey, very sweet. She will help your leg.'

The rest of the family, except for Papa, came in, kissed their aunt and sat around the room. Mohamed switched on the television.

I smiled back, as Aunt Fatma sat down to inspect my ankle. She prodded it gently all over, then took a tube and a bandage from her big handbag. She spread ointment over the ankle. It was cool and soothing. Then came the bandage, which she applied expertly. I could feel the benefit immediately. She tied up the two ends and gently laid my ankle back down.

'That feels so much better. Thank you very much.'

Aunt Fatma then went to chat to her brother in his bedroom, while we continued to watch the film in the sitting-room. Again, raised voices filtered through. After ten minutes, she returned to watch the end of the film with us, drinking a glass of black, sweet tea. She sat next to me and kept patting my knee in a reassuring way. As soon as the credits rolled, she stood up to leave. She looked pointedly at me and burst forth with a stream of Arabic.

Salma smiled. 'She has spoken with Papa. She say to Papa no be angry with you. She say him that you don't know how we do things. She say you are a good girl. She say he will listen to her.'

'She's lovely,' I thought, as I kissed her goodbye.

Omar had been glancing across at me throughout the film, and I made sure to acknowledge him each time with a smile. There would have been so much to talk about if only he had been able to speak English.

Mohamed switched off the television, said goodnight and went to his room. To my surprise, Tarek came through dressed in trousers and a shirt, kissed his mother and left.

'My brother Tarek has a wife, Mervette. He goes to her now.'

'Does he live here or with his wife?'

'He lives with Mervette. He comes every week one day to be with his father,' explained Salma.

Omar then bent over to me and looked right into my eyes.

'Good night.'

'Good night,' I replied, looking right back.

'Come with me to sleep,' said Salma. We made our way to the back bedroom. 'You rest now. I must pray.'

She left to wash, returning with a thin veil draped over her head. Her feet were bare and I saw that she had also washed them. She took a rug, laid it out in front of the wardrobe and stood at one end of it, facing the wardrobe to begin her prayers.

I watched, fascinated, as she knelt, touched the rug with her head several times, stood up again and bowed, whispering prayers to herself.

Upon finishing, she went to a cupboard and brought out a large book embossed with gold and wrapped in a towel.

'This is the Koran. My prayers come from here. See.'

She placed the book on my knee. Gingerly, I tried to open it.

'No, no, like this.'

Salma opened the book from the left side. I stared, confused as to why such an important book would open the wrong way round.

'We write Arabic this way, from right to left.' She traced the lines of print with her fingers. 'It is our holy book.'

'We have the Bible,' I told her. 'Why do you put it in this?' I held up the towel.

She foraged for a moment in the dictionary.

'We must respect the Koran, and we must wash when we touch it or read it. We must keep it clean and safe always.'

I closed the book and watched her carefully wrap it up and place it back on the top shelf of the cupboard. Then she removed the rug from the floor.

'This is a prayer mat. I pray with this five times. I must wash before I pray. It is called *wudu*. It makes me clean for Allah.'

'So why do you pray to the wardrobe?'

'No, no, Jacky, not the wardrobe. I pray to Mecca, where the prophet Mohamed was born. It is in the east. This wardrobe is east.' She laughed. 'Today I teach you about Islam, and that I do not pray to wardrobes.'

This had taken a lot for Salma to explain in English, and she was looking tired. She took a *galabeya* from the shelf and handed it to me.

'We sleep now.'

I washed, changed into the *galabeya*, and lay on the bed beside her.

Even the beds were different. Instead of sheets or duvets, there was an eiderdown on the mattress with a blanket if you needed to cover up. There wasn't any air-conditioning, but instead, the fans kept the worst of the heat at bay. Now they were switched off, it soon became hot and clammy in the room.

'You will be ill if you sleep with it on,' explained Salma.

I lay back, staring at the ceiling, considering the events of the day. Something was happening to me. I had forgotten all about Dave and everything else. All I thought about was Omar.

'I'm daydreaming about him constantly. When he walks into a room, I hold my breath. When he leaves, I wonder where he's going.'

I closed my eyes in an effort to sleep. 'I wonder if he's thinking about me now?'

Aunt Fatma had certainly worked her magic on Papa. I awoke the next morning to a short rap on the door. It was Mama, smiling broadly and carrying a tray. A large bruise had formed at the top of one cheek and extended down to her chin, all mottled black and blue. I noticed that she had made no attempt to disguise it.

She set the tray down on the end of the bed and looked at me.

'Good morning. Tea. We say *Shay bi lebban*.' She picked up the glass of milky white tea. '*Eshrebby*. Drink.'

Her knowledge of English was quite good, but she didn't trust herself to use full sentences without supplying the Arabic as well. She now turned to Salma and spoke in Arabic.

'Papa says you must eat breakfast with the family in one hour. You are welcome,' she said.

Mama was delighted to bring this news and her bruise was forgotten as she hugged me tightly. Papa's word was very important in the running of this household.

I sat up, smiling. 'Good morning.'

Shay bi lebban turned out to be tea with milk, highly sweetened. Mama had brought two glasses for Salma and me, with two large pieces of sponge cake. This was a typical wake-up breakfast, and the only time they put milk in the tea.

'I don't need sugar in my tea, Salma.'

'Yes, you need it. It is very good. It will make you strong.'

I realised that the possibility of drinking tea without sugar in this household was very slim.

My ankle felt a lot better, although I still wasn't ready to put any pressure on it. The rest had certainly got rid of the dull ache that had been there the previous day.

After a wash and change, I was helped into Papa's bedroom where I sat on the bed with him, Mama and Magda. Mohamed appeared, dressed in smart jeans with a collarless shirt not tucked in, looking very casual. He had two packages wrapped in newspaper. He had been out somewhere to buy these.

Newspaper was spread over the eiderdown. One package contained a saucepan with brown beans in it. They were larger than baked beans, but looked similar, in a brown sauce. The other had small, round, deep-fried balls of chickpeas. Omar arrived with fresh bread, still warm from the oven.

'Good morning. We eat,' pronounced Papa, in English.

I waited to see exactly how to proceed. I didn't want to blow this second chance.

'This is breakfast in bed with a difference,' I thought.

The beans were scooped into pieces of torn-off bread. The fried balls were eaten by hand, or in bread. Inside, they were bright green. I managed a couple of these, but the beans tasted so totally different from anything I had ever eaten. They were very bland and not to my taste.

Salma did try to translate for me, but was unable to locate the English in a dictionary. The beans were called *fool*, and the fried balls, *tarmayer*.

Every bit of food was consumed, with lots of water. The men then prepared for their prayers, which they performed together in one room. The girls and Mama washed after the men and went to pray in another room.

The sun was streaming into the sitting-room. I hobbled in

and sat on a chair, watching the world go by from the open window.

The next five days went by in a whirl. While we made daily inquiries at the youth hostel, there was no news of Dave, and the family took it upon themselves to adopt me. They were so hospitable, putting themselves out to make me comfortable and enjoy their country.

Omar was the chauffeur for the excursions, which made them all the more attractive. That first day, he and Salma took me into the centre of Cairo, where there were the department stores and huge buildings I had looked for on the bus. Bursting with traffic, horns blaring constantly from all directions, the noise was deafening.

We stopped to visit the flea market area of Khanin Khalili. It was full of stalls and shops selling *galabeyas*, bags, stuffed camels, miniature pyramids and gold jewellery.

'Hi there, baby. Wanna come inside? I give you very good bargain.'

'It is really very expensive,' whispered Salma, shaking her head at the man and guiding me away. 'Just look. If you like anything we can take you to another place and buy it cheap for you.'

It was like Aladdin's cave, glittering with jewellery and fancy, ingrained, carved furniture and trinkets. Tinny Arabian music blared out from loudspeakers, and every so often there were tiny coffee shops with men sitting outside smoking bubble pipes and playing backgammon.

It took a long time to walk round, due to my ankle. We returned to the car, and drove on to a cafe in a large square.

'This is famous for the rice pudding. We will eat some.'

Big posters advertised the product, *Roz bi lebban*. It was cold, in a little pot, and utterly disgusting. It was embarrassing, but I didn't really like the taste of any of the Egyptian dishes I'd tried. Now I sat with a dish in front of me, miserably nibbling cold rice from the end of a stained teaspoon.

After a siesta back at the flat, the whole family piled into the car for a trip to the pyramids at Giza. This was the first time I had seen Mama and Papa dressed in normal clothes. Mama wore a flimsy, transparent white veil and looked very smart in a blue dress. Papa wore a shirt and trousers and looked very business-like.

I was expecting the pyramids to be in the middle of the desert, as they are usually portrayed in photographs or books. But instead they were just at the top of a hill on the outskirts of the city, Giza. This was just another suburb of Cairo, to be found at the end of a very long, straight road called *Shera el Haram*, or Pyramid Street.

The car began to climb a slope. The Mena House Hotel stood at the bottom of the slope and the pyramids were at the top, where it levelled out into a plateau. The Sphinx was awe-inspiring. In real life it was huge, sitting on guard, in front of the three pyramids. Tourists were milling around, with Egyptian boys riding horses bareback and men with camels offering rides.

Huge spotlights lit up each of the pyramids at night and now they glowed in the light of the late afternoon sun. We approached the first, the Great Pyramid, *Cheops*. It was extraordinary in its greatness. The sheer size was unbelievable. The entrance was on the side facing us.

'Wow! How on earth did they manage to build these so many years ago?' I exclaimed.

'I don't know,' replied Salma. 'It is, how you say, a mystery. Come, we go up.'

She took my hand and tried to help me up onto the first level of stones. They were at chest height, and it was not easy. I eventually hauled myself up and looked at the vast number of other levels that made up this pyramid, each level as tall as the last. Geometrically precise in every way, it stretched up for miles. I was standing on one of the wonders of the world, a piece of history. It was a very humbling experience, and it made me feel very small indeed.

I was in a different world on this plateau. Up here, I had left behind the trees, shops and civilisation at the bottom of the slope. This was a kingdom in the desert. Looking out, away from the slope, there was just sand stretching for miles, with the three pyramids standing majestically in the foreground. It was a fantastic sight.

'Can we go inside?' I asked Salma.

'Your leg is no good for this, I think,' she replied.

'Oh please, I'll try hard to make it.' I really wanted to see inside the chambers.

'Omar!' Salma called her brother, and he was immediately

at my side. He raised his arms and I leaned down into him to reach the floor. He took my hand and held it tightly.

'Come,' he whispered.

I was in heaven. This was the most romantic place in the whole world, and the most attractive man in the world was holding my hand.

It was in fact easier than I had anticipated. There were banisters to hold on to as we crept up and down the narrow corridors, all well lit with electric lights. It was very steep in parts, but there were wooden ramps.

We had to bend double in places, as the ceilings were low. Eventually, the passage straightened out and led to a rough chamber. We then made our way to the heart of the pyramid, and this proved to be the most difficult part. It had been relatively easy on my ankle, shuffling downwards, but creeping upwards put pressure on all the wrong places and all the pain came shooting back whenever I tried to move.

'I can't,' I moaned, moving back into the chamber. 'If I can't go upwards, then I'll never get out of here. What can I do?'

I had forgotten that Omar could not understand me. But he put his arm round me anyway, drew me towards him, and wiped my hair from my face. As I leaned against him, he gently lifted my face and kissed me.

I forgot all about my ankle in that moment. I simply melted as I kissed him back.

'Sorry,' he drew away.

'No, not sorry,' I stroked his cheek and smiled.

I had suddenly found renewed strength, and decided to try

again. With our hands locked tightly together, we began the narrow ascent until the path straightened and led into the Queen's Chamber with its smooth, polished walls. We passed through and on to the Grand Gallery, which was even more impressive. It ran upwards, but we were no longer cramped. The ceilings were much higher, narrowing at the top. The Grand Gallery wound its way up to the King's Chamber, a massive room, lined with smooth, black granite. At one end was the sarcophagus, again made of granite. But it wasn't smooth at all. All around the edge it was chipped and battered.

The physical closeness of Omar as we made our way out of the Great Pyramid made it easier for me to cope with my ankle. He made everything better, as far as I was concerned.

We rejoined the others and sat together in that magical place until sunset, when we made our way home.

Later, while Salma was in the bathroom, I was lying in bed when Omar quickly nipped in and kissed me.

'Goodnight, *habibti*,' he whispered.

'I must ask Salma to translate that sometime,' I thought, 'although I think I can guess.'

10

Fatal Attraction

The following day, Salma went to school. Omar drove Mama, Magda and me to see Aunt Fatma and her family. She had two daughters, who practised their English with me, while Aunt Fatma put my ankle in a bowl of water and essential oils to soak. She then bound it with a fresh bandage. The swelling was definitely going down.

That evening, when Salma returned, Omar drove us along the banks of the Nile, pointing out the posh hotels, Shepherds, the Meridian, Nile Hilton and Sheraton Gezira. The feluccas with their white, square sails looked beautiful, sailing this way and that, passing the Nile buses, full of passengers. We stopped at the riverside. I could see couples together in the restaurants, their laughter drifting across the water, their faces bright in the candlelight.

I threw myself into the experience of being in this country with this family. I barely gave Dave a thought. Omar was good enough to visit the hostel every evening, but there was never any news.

The next day, Papa did not feel very well. Salma went to school, leaving Mama and Magda to care for him. Omar tried to speak English, but kept introducing French words.

'French, do you speak French?' I asked him, also in French. His eyes widened.

'Yes, not so well, but enough,' he answered, in very passable French.

'At last. We can speak to each other.' This was such a relief. I was good at French, having studied hard at school and spent the summer months with my French penfriend for several years on the trot.

'Jacky, I love you.'

'You mean *like*. I like you too.'

'No. I mean *love*. I love you, Jacky. Let's go out, just you and I.'

We took the car and drove to the zoo. I was able to wander around almost normally. Omar draped his hand casually around my shoulders and kept pulling me into bushes or behind animal cages to kiss me. We stopped for a Coke, laughing at the baboons, asking each other all sorts of questions.

'How do I ask for water in Arabic?'

'That's easy. Just say to the waiter, "*Fee myer, min fadlek*."'

The waiter approached and brought the water I had asked for. It felt great to be understood. I kept asking Omar this word and that word, determined to use Arabic whenever the opportunity arose.

The time flew by. Omar was so attentive, caring, interested. He told me he loved me over and again.

'I can't believe he likes me so much,' I thought, gazing at him as he drove us home. He was so handsome, his skin fairer than his brothers', with delicate freckles on his forehead and cheeks, his hair a dark shade of auburn, the wavy curls framing his carved cheekbones and sensuous lips. His eyes, a deep, dark brown that looked right into my soul, were full of yearning, passion and adoration. When he smiled, they crinkled at the edges and turned my stomach to jelly.

'I know he doesn't really love me, but it feels so good when he tells me. I don't ever want this holiday to end.'

As we entered the flat, laughing together, Salma appeared, her face drawn and worried. She pulled angrily at Omar's shirt, speaking very fast, in Arabic. I assumed it was an everyday, trivial problem. I was getting used to the dramatic gestures and the shouting. It was impossible, without understanding the actual words, to discern a quarrel from a chat.

But Salma was genuinely upset. She came to see me a few minutes later in the bedroom.

'My brother is very bad, Jacky. I am angry with him. Here in Egypt, a girl does not go alone with men. She must be with brothers or sisters. She cannot go alone. Her family will be angry.'

Papa had recovered and we all ate together that evening. All, that is, except for Omar. He was nowhere to be seen. I realised that he had made a big mistake in taking me out, and must now be paying the price.

Papa kept his eyes on me, but he needn't have bothered. I could hardly eat a thing. I was desperately unhappy, almost panicking at the thought of never seeing him again.

'Is this love?' I wondered. I didn't believe such a thing as love at first sight really existed, but what other explanation could there be? My feelings didn't make any sense, but they were very real and very powerful.

I slept fitfully, tossing and turning until morning. The rest hadn't helped. I felt just as miserable as I had the night before.

'Jacky, good morning. Today I not go to school. We all go to Port Said and *Iskandrayer*. Especially for you, Jacky. I'm so happy.' Salma offered me tea and cake as she explained, 'I love to see the sea.'

Her enthusiasm was infectious and, despite myself, I smiled and chatted while we dressed. My ankle was almost better, and I could now slip my trainer on, which gave much more support than the flimsy sandal I had been wearing.

I wanted to ask after Omar but didn't dare to, sensing the seriousness of his offence. So my heart soared when he appeared to drive us all to the ports of Alexandria and Port Said.

The road was long, straight and boring. Villages gave way to desert. Lorries and cars flew along at tremendous speeds, and we passed two accidents on the way. Both involved white Peugeots. This wasn't symbolic in any way; all long-distance taxis were white Peugeot estates, and it was by far the most popular car in Egypt.

At the scene of the first accident, passengers were sitting in the dust wailing, some were lying injured at the side of the road, luggage had toppled off the overloaded roof, and there were oranges spilling out of a sack into our path. A man stood with his arm out, trying to flag us down. Omar didn't even glance in his direction, but swerved to avoid the fruit and continue on.

'Why didn't we stop?' I asked Salma.

'We can do nothing. We are full,' she stated.

Omar concentrated on driving, although we managed to exchange a couple of private glances via the mirror.

Alexandria was a huge port, the roads running along the coast, with wonderful beaches with fine, white sand. We wandered along the seafront up to the port and went to see the giant obelisk, Cleopatra's Needle. It was a flying visit, however. After a picnic lunch, we set off for Port Said. This was a duty-free port, so there were customs to drive through. It was a much smaller port, with narrow streets full of market traders and little shops. The family spent a lot of money buying clothes, shoes, perfume and household bits. There were many imported items available, such as fake designer labels, Gucci bags, Versace scarves, football shirts and imitation Nike trainers.

We stopped at a cafe for *ahwa*, black, sweet coffee in tiny cups, and *baclava*, a sweet pastry with lots of syrup. The coffee was thick and very strong and the pastry was far too sickly, but I ate it without complaint. I was getting used to forcing food and drink into my mouth to avoid insulting Papa.

It had been a tiring day, and I fell asleep on the way back. Later, Omar motioned for me to join him in the bedroom, as everyone was watching the television.

'Jacky, I can't go on like this. I want to be with you. I need you. I love you so much.' He stroked my cheek as he said this, looking deep into my eyes.

'I want to be with you, too, but what can we do? I cannot make Papa angry with me again.'

'Jacky, my love, I never want us to be apart. Will you marry me?'

I had been shocked when he had said he loved me, but this was too much. I laughed.

'Omar, be serious. We don't have much time. Someone is bound to come looking for us.'

'I have never been so serious about anything. Jacky, do you love me?'

Without hesitation, I knew the answer. 'Yes. I love you, Omar.'

He hugged me to him. 'Then marry me. Stay here with me forever. Be my wife. Have my children. Never ever leave me.'

'You are completely mad. Of course we can't get married. What about my life in England, and my family?'

I thought momentarily of Dave, but he was no longer part of the equation. I had definitely moved on. He was now the past.

I sighed and shook my head. 'No, Omar, I cannot marry you. You will have to think of some other way for us to spend time together. Let's go back now, before anyone gets suspicious.'

The following day, Omar left the house in the morning. Salma and I took a stroll up the street to another aunt's house, where we were made very welcome and drank 7-Up. On the way back, I stopped at a kiosk to buy some postcards and stamps.

'You need to put the card in an envelope to be sure it gets there,' said Salma.

'That's silly. I might as well write a letter.'

She shrugged.

'When in Rome,' I thought, and bought some envelopes as well.

When we returned, there was still no sign of Omar. In the middle of the afternoon, he returned. I was alone, writing postcards.

He knelt down beside me, taking my hand and kissing it.

'Jacky, I am nothing without you. I don't want to live unless we can be husband and wife. Please say you will marry me.'

'Oh Omar, it cannot be. We must not even think about it,' I started, but he interrupted.

'You do not believe me? You do not think I am serious? I will show you just how serious I am about this. Come.' He pulled me gently to my feet and led me into the front sitting-room. 'Wait here. I am going to speak to Papa, and sort everything out, right now.'

He left me alone, stunned. How could he do this? Papa would be furious whatever Omar said to him. I shuddered. I had already witnessed Papa's wrath once, and I certainly couldn't see him laughing at this.

It was peaceful in that front sitting-room. The television had not yet been switched on in there, and was still covered by a prayer mat. I could hear the other televisions in the bedrooms. *The Little House on the Prairie* with Arabic subtitles was on. If only my life was as simple, I thought.

The peace was suddenly shattered by the *adhan*, the call to prayer. By now, I could almost imitate it to the word, complete with warble: *Allahhhhhhh akbar*, 'God is great.'

'Could I live here, with these customs, and make a new life among these people?' I wondered. Did I want to get married to Omar? I knew I didn't want to leave him. When I returned to England, our paths would never cross again. It would turn into the classic holiday romance.

The *adhan* finished and peace was restored. My thoughts began to run away with me. 'And anyway, supposing I said yes, how on earth could we manage everything, with my family virtually on the other side of the world? No, it's madness to consider. After all, exactly what do I know about him anyway?'

I knew he was a Moslem, who took his religion seriously. All the family prayed and learned *suras* from the Koran by heart, the foundation on which they build the rest of their lives. Could I live with that?

As Omar was fighting for me with Papa, I was wrestling with myself in the sitting-room.

'There's no way on earth Papa will agree to his son marrying a non-Moslem and a foreigner at that. So there is no decision to be made, because it will be made for us. Of course Papa is right. What on earth was I thinking of? It's ridiculous to even think of marrying a man I hardly know. I know nothing of his culture, language or past. How would I explain all this to Mum and Dad? I am an only child. My parents would be terribly hurt. They would never understand. No, absolutely and finally.'

* * *

Two hours later, Omar appeared with a defiant look on his face. I stood up to meet him.

'I *will* marry you, Jacky, with or without my father's permission.'

He wrapped his arms around me. I breathed in his now familiar smell of Paco Rabanne and hugged him tightly.

'Will you marry me?' he whispered.

'Yes, yes, yes,' I replied, seduced by the intensity of the moment.

'But it will never happen,' a little voice inside my head whispered.

11

Proposals

Omar went back to speak to Papa, wearing a fixed, determined expression. I had never seen him like this before. We could hear lots of shouting, then silence, then shouting again. I sat listening, feeling tense. Time stood still. I looked down and realised I had bitten all of the nails on one hand down to the quick, something I never did.

The family did not interfere. Mama, Magda and Salma changed into outdoor clothes and took me out for an evening stroll along the banks of the Nile. There were restaurants and cafes along the riverbank, and an open-air cinema. We walked along the wide pavement and sat on the low wall that ran alongside.

Feluccas idled their way across the river, their tall, white sails bending into the breeze, the multicoloured evening sky creating a magnificent backdrop for these striking boats with their angular shapes and their lights twinkling across the water. I watched them gliding gracefully amidst other river traffic – river buses, fishing boats, dinghies – and imagined Omar and me sailing away on our romantic honeymoon.

Every fifty yards, under the tall palm trees, traders stood

with their barrows selling sunflower seeds, hot yams or barbecued corn on the cob. Magda ordered corn for us all and we sat and watched the old man turn them again and again on the hot coals until the yellow maize turned to black. I stared at his wrinkled face, full of cracks and furrows like a walnut, and at the faded cloth wrapped around his head for a turban, soiled with smoke. He brushed the hot coals several times with his hands, yet never flinched. His hands were hardy and blackened by smoke. After ten minutes the corn was ready. The old man lifted them off the hot coals and wrapped the end of each one in newspaper for us to eat. The smoky aroma it produced was totally intoxicating.

'Mmm, these are so delicious.' I blew on mine to cool it down more quickly. 'In England, we put these into a pan of water and boil them.'

Salma burst into peals of laughter and translated to the others. Mama simply refused to believe me.

'She says the English cannot be so stupid.'

Mama got up and walked along to the next trader. As we caught up with her, the man was twisting pieces of newspaper into cones and filling them with sunflower seeds. Mama bought three packets and we started for home. I assumed they were for a pet, although I had seen no evidence of any animals in the flat.

'Do you have a pet? A hamster, perhaps?'

Salma grimaced at my question. 'Agh, no. They are like rats. We do not keep pets like this in Egypt. Instead, we visit the zoo.'

'Then why do you buy the bags of seeds?'

'*Lib*? We eat them. They are very good. Look, you try some.'

She ran up to her mother, who handed her one of the cones. Salma shook several *lib* out into her hand, biting each one and taking the seed out with her tongue. It looked really easy. It wasn't. No matter how I tried, I couldn't get the seed out of the shell, although when Salma gave me one, it tasted good.

We were all laughing and enjoying our walk. As we rounded the last corner, Omar burst out of the building, running as fast as he could towards us. He was with us in seconds, picked me up and swung me round, gabbling on in Arabic.

'Omar.' His mother brought him back to his senses and he set me down, before flinging his arms round Mama.

She looked angry at first, but then her face broke into a smile as she held Omar's face between both hands and kissed him twice on each cheek. She began speaking quickly and excitedly.

I looked at Salma. 'What is she saying?'

'She says *Mabrouk ebni, elfe mabrouk*. Congratulations my son, a thousand congratulations.'

Magda was suddenly kissing me, babbling on in Arabic. And then it hit me like a ton of bricks. Papa had agreed. Omar had got his way. I felt weak at the knees, and held on to Salma. I thought I was going to faint. My mouth was dry and my head was swimming. I stared in disbelief, first at Mama and then at Omar. What had happened to change his mind? A mere three hours earlier, there had been no chance of him agreeing to the marriage.

Suddenly I was afraid. I wasn't completely sure how I felt about this turn of events. I should have been happy that I was now free to go ahead and marry an Egyptian man I had known for barely a week, but I wasn't sure. It was happening so quickly that I could barely keep track of my own feelings. I was bundled back into the flat in the midst of their excitement, a flurry of emotions racing through me.

Papa ventured out of his room to shake my hand, kiss me on both cheeks and congratulate me. Mohamed shyly shook my hand and bent to kiss my cheeks.

'Yes, he can do this. You will be his sister.' Salma laughed delightedly at the thought. Mohamed blushed and disappeared into his room.

Mama and Papa began discussing arrangements with Omar. As I couldn't understand a word they were saying, Salma and I left them to it. I could certainly do with a good night's sleep after all this.

In bed, I tried to imagine spending the rest of my life in this foreign Moslem land. So far, things had been very different but not necessarily worse than life at home. It would be a real challenge. But I was confident that Omar would always be there to help me through, and as long as we were together, what else really mattered?

'Yes,' I decided, 'I can do this. More than that, I can make a brilliant life out here for both of us.'

Our impending marriage overrode any plans the family may have had for the next few days, as the two sisters and Mama fussed over me, taking measurements, choosing underwear, shoes, experimenting with a thousand hairstyles and different types of make-up.

Omar was in and out, fetching and carrying, but always finding the time to make me feel like the luckiest girl in the world, explaining everything that was happening.

'We must marry here, in this flat. I will bring chairs, food and drink. I must visit relatives and friends to invite them. I want to tell the whole world, I am so happy. I have many jobs, and so little time. We marry in two days.'

'And two days after that, I fly back to London,' I thought.

We had arranged that I would still return to London to explain everything in person to my side of the family. I could then arrange to fly back when I had sorted out all my affairs.

The front door slammed behind him as Mama called, 'Come, Jacky.'

I went through to the front bedroom and sat on the bed. As Mama strode towards me, I suddenly felt very intimidated. Uncertainty and doubt washed over me like a tidal wave. This dip in confidence occurred every time Omar went away.

'Not here. Come.'

Mama struggled to find the words, so she grasped my arm and half dragged me into the kitchen. They were boiling sugar and lemon juice in a small pan.

'*Hellewa*. For you,' Salma said with a smile.

It had a strong, sickly smell. When she removed it from the heat and stirred it, the texture changed from a liquid to a stretchy, gooey paste, which looked and smelt awful.

'For me? I really don't feel hungry, thank you. I don't think I could eat anything at the moment,' I told her.

Salma giggled as she translated to Mama and Magda, who both burst out laughing.

'You are very funny, Jacky. I want very much to be sisters.' Mama turned out the *hellewa* into a plastic bowl.

'You must go to the bedroom with us now,' said Salma, taking my hand. 'Take all your clothes away, please.'

'Oh, now I understand,' I thought, '*hellewa* isn't something to eat after all. It must be some sort of body treatment, like an all-over facial. How wonderful. I am going to enjoy every minute of this.'

I removed my clothes, lay on the bed, relaxed and closed my eyes.

A burning sensation ripped through my arm, as if someone had poured a kettle of boiling water on it. I leapt up in agony. But instead of a kettle, there was merely a portion of the sticky substance smeared over my upper arm.

'Jacky, sit. Don't worry. Magda will now pull it off,' Salma soothed. 'It won't hurt.'

Magda reached over and with a slight movement of her wrist, ripped off the *hellewa*. Intense pain seared through my body, filling me with fear and determination. I jumped off the bed and tried to flee from the room, but immediately came up against Mama blocking the door, shouting and pointing at my state of undress. I was shaking, so I sat down again. Salma and Magda sat on either side and gently put their arms around me.

'Jacky, you are to be the wife of an Egyptian man,' Salma explained. 'Before you marry, when you are a girl, you do not have to do this. But when you become a woman, your husband must see you very clean. You must take all this off.' She stroked my arm and leg to show me what she meant. 'Every single hair on your body must go for your husband to want you and love you. You want to make Omar happy, yes?'

I sat between them, stunned. 'This is just too much to ask,' I thought. 'If the women have to get rid of all their hair, then why not the men too? I suppose hair on males is supposed to be attractive. Women certainly get the raw end of the deal.'

'No, Salma. I don't understand how Omar would be happy for me to do that. He fell in love with me with hair. He can marry me with hair.'

As she translated, I could feel the tension mounting. What would they do if I didn't conform to their ways? Mama shouted and I waited.

'She says hair is ugly, and it is how we do things here. She says her son loves you, but would not be happy in his heart to see you with hair on your wedding night.'

I reached up to free my long, thick, blonde hair, and shook it out over both my shoulders.

'Salma, I have had long hair all my life. How can you ask me to remove it? It scares me.'

She looked puzzled. 'But you don't need to cut the hair here.' She pointed to my head. 'Just on the body.'

Maybe it was the relief, but upon hearing this little conversation between us, both Mama and Magda laughed so much that tears streamed down their cheeks.

I didn't share their humour. 'So, I don't have to shave my head, but I still have to go through this *hellewa* process,' I thought.

I looked at their arms. Mama's were ultra smooth. But their skin was considerably darker than mine and looked somehow stronger. I turned my attention to the part of my arm where Magda had ripped off the *hellewa*. It was glowing and stinging. I made an instant decision.

'Just rip it off quickly, like a plaster,' I told Salma, lying back once more and resigning myself to the whole strange operation. The pain came in waves. The absolute worst part was under my arms, which began to bleed. At this point, Magda stopped.

'You shower now. It is good.' Salma was pleased with the progress being made.

I did as I was told, willingly this time. I stood under the cool, gushing water, feeling my body tingle until it was eventually soothed. Covered only by a towel, I returned to the bedroom and collapsed on the bed. My skin was blotchy all over.

Already I was missing Omar. I closed my eyes.

My left leg was suddenly yanked open, and before I could protest, Magda had slapped a large dollop of *hellewa* between my legs.

I tried in vain to sit up. Big Mama held my legs firmly apart, Salma pressed down on my shoulders and Magda bent to rip the hellish *hellewa* off.

This time, my scream brought them to a startled halt. I saw my chance and jumped off the bed with such a threatening look in my eye that they backed away and left me. I found a chair, wedged it firmly under the door handle and threw myself back onto the bed sobbing.

'So this is what they meant by removing all the hair except for on your head. I never dreamt they'd go that far,' I thought miserably.

Hours later, I opened the door to a concerned Omar.

'What is it? What has happened?'

'Nothing really. A little problem, that's all,' I replied quietly, looking down at the floor. 'Could I have a pair of scissors, please? And then I would like to have some time on my own.'

'But I want to help you. Please tell me what's wrong.'

'It's a woman thing. Not for men to know about. Okay?'

'You haven't changed your mind, have you? Please just tell me that.'

'No. I haven't changed my mind.'

We kissed and he brought some scissors, leaving reluctantly.

'Now for the clean-up operation,' I muttered, wondering what would be the best way to go about it. I found a compact mirror in a bedside drawer and positioned it carefully to get the best view. For the next hour, I grappled with pubic hair, scissors and *hellewa*, which now had a texture like putty. Attempting to extricate such a sticky mess was a miserable process. I eventually gave up in exasperation. In the tiny mirror, I could plainly see the awful effects of my surgery.

The end result was even worse than before I had started.

'Oh God, what am I going to do now? It's my wedding night in a couple of days. I want to feel beautiful, sexy, attractive and ultra-feminine. Instead, I'm a freak.'

This was the nightmare of all nightmares. The ultimate complex. One side with pubic hair and one side without. I just couldn't cope with the thought.

12

I Do

Outside, the light was fading as the sun went down. The muezzin began the now-familiar *adhan*, calling all Moslems to prayer, and I could hear the family on the other side of the bedroom door shouting to one another as they prepared to pray. I felt isolated and very much a stranger. Without a clue as to how to resolve such an embarrassing problem, I did the only thing left to do.

I lay down and cried myself to sleep.

I awoke to find myself in bed beside Salma, who had joined me while I had been sleeping. The idea that everyone would have their own bed would not even have occurred to the family, and few women in Egypt ever had such a privilege. I was wearing a *galabeya*. The events of the previous day rushed into my mind, and I wondered if it had all been a dream. I held up my arm to the sunlight squeezing through the tiny gap in the shutters.

'Smooth as silk,' I murmured, stroking it up and down. 'Now for the big question.'

I gently lifted the blanket and slipped a hand under the *galabeya* between my legs. My heart sank. There was nothing but sticky stubble on one side and smooth pubic hair on the other. It hadn't been a dream. I was horrified. For a moment, clinging to the idea that it had been a dream had given me fresh hope.

'I have to do *something*. There's no way I am going ahead with any marriage like this. I'll just have to find a way of removing all the hair, but without the pain.'

My ankle was much stronger now, enabling me to stomp to the bathroom for a wash. At least I managed to scrub off all the remaining *hellewa*.

At breakfast, Omar was very attentive and gorgeous. All my worries were swept aside as we laughed and chatted.

'Are you happy?'

'Only when I'm with you. Do you have a lot to do today?'

'I must sort out my suit. I need rings, someone to make photographs. Yes, there are many things to do.'

'Can I go to a chemist with someone today? Will you take me?'

'Salma will walk with you later. What do you want? Can I get it for you?'

'No, I would prefer to go with Salma. You sort out your suit.'

He disappeared to dress. As soon as he'd left, I pounced on Salma, almost begging her to take me to a chemist there and then.

'But the dress is coming this morning,' she protested.

'Can we go before it arrives? Please, Salma, I really need you to take me.'

* * *

We hurried out into the dusty street. I shielded my eyes against the glaring sun, which was in dazzling contrast to the shadowy confines of the flat.

The pharmacy was on the next corner. The glass doors were covered in dust with Arabic graffiti drawn all over them. Inside a thin man was standing behind a wide counter, serving a young woman. Her daughter stared at us from behind her mother's long skirt. An electric fan blew the air around our faces, bringing with it the faint smell of mint. I stood quietly to one side to let them pass, as Salma bought the cream I was so desperate for. Walking back, she took the cream out of the bag and examined the box disapprovingly.

'Four pounds, seventy-five piastres. That is ridiculously expensive. And not as good as *hellewa*. Only the foreigners use this sort of stuff.'

'I am a foreigner, Salma,' I replied quietly.

Within half an hour, we were back at the flat and I had locked myself in the bathroom. I held up the minute tube of hair removal cream. Of one thing I was sure: it was going to be worth every last piastre.

Frenzied preparations continued all day. Two wedding dresses were presented to me to try on for size. The first one belonged to Mervette, the wife of Tarek, Omar's elder brother. He brought it round and congratulated me.

The dress took my breath away. It was absolutely stunning, but a size too small. Reluctantly, I gave it back, although I knew I'd never look as good in a different dress.

I was wrong. Mohamed then arrived with a cousin's wedding dress, which fitted perfectly. It wasn't all flouncy or layered, but cut simply, emphasising all the right places. It was flattering, stylish and elegant. I was surprised, as Mama had shown me a huge folder containing wedding dresses in different styles, which one of her relatives had compiled. She was a seamstress, and made all the clothes for the family. The one thing they all had in common was the fussiness, the frills, the metres of lace, the layers and the high necks. Yet this dress was not at all like that. In fact it could have been an English wedding dress.

It was sent down to the *maquaggi*, the ironing man. When we had gone to the chemist, I had noticed his tiny shop below the pavement, with steps leading down into it. He was using an old-fashioned iron that he heated up on an open fire.

'I hope he won't burn the dress,' I said.

'He is an excellent *maquaggi*. He has been doing this all of his life,' replied Salma.

'In England, we have irons at home and we iron our own clothes on special boards,' I explained.

'Here in Egypt, it is usually a man's job. We never iron things for ourselves.'

As the day progressed, shoes were sorted out to fit me, my eyebrows were plucked and my nails were attended to. I insisted on clear varnish and we had a practice run of the hair and make-up, as I didn't want to end up resembling some sort of painted doll.

Caught up in the flurry of activities, I was swept along with the mood of the others. There wasn't a spare moment for reflection, and I fell into bed that night exhausted.

It simply hadn't occurred to me to ask where we would be living, or what we would be living on. Omar was a student at Cairo University and not earning any money on a regular basis.

As the wedding day dawned, Mama kept me in the bedroom, to be made up and have my hair done. I sat nervously on a chair while they fussed over me, drinking tea. Salma went to see how the men were getting on. She returned after only a few minutes.

'Omar is so excited, Jacky. He is changed and ready. He looks beautiful.'

There was a knock on the door. Mama and Magda rushed to open it, and brought the freshly ironed wedding gown for me to wear. They slipped it over my head, zipped it up and I was ready.

'Don't leave the room.' Salma wagged her finger at me, as the three of them went to change and get themselves ready.

I stood up and positioned the window so that I could see my reflection.

'Wow! You don't look so bad after all.'

I twirled around, enjoying the feel of the silk on my body. Even my ankle was cured. Soon the others returned, dressed. Salma had a tiara and white veil in her hand.

'You will meet many people today,' she informed me, fixing the tiara in place with grips. 'They will all come up to you. The women will kiss you on each cheek. You will kiss them back.

The men will shake your hand. You must not look into the eyes of the men. They will say, "*Mabrouk*", and you must reply, '*Shokran*'. There. That's finished.'

She stepped back to admire her handiwork.

'What does "*mabrouk*" mean?'

'"Congratulations". Are you ready?'

I was ready.

Followed by Magda and Salma, I made my way along the narrow corridor, into the front sitting-room. Omar was standing in attendance, holding his arms out to greet me.

'You are beautiful,' he whispered, wiping away a tear from his eye, before indicating that I should sit on one of the two large chairs placed at one end of the room.

Mohamed switched on a cassette, and romantic Arabian music filled the room. Guests began to arrive, all dressed up in their finery.

'*Mabrouk, mabrouk.*'

'*Shokran.*'

After a while, my nerves disappeared, and I began to enjoy this ritual. The guests were genuinely pleased to meet me and congratulate us. Their high spirits rubbed off on me, and I was soon smiling and nodding enthusiastically at the comments they made; not that I had a clue what they were talking about.

About an hour into the celebrations, the imam arrived to bless us. He wore a white crocheted hat, and a white *galabeya* with trousers beneath. He had a grey moustache and wore glasses with thick black frames, making him appear very intimidating.

He could not officially marry us, as I was not a Moslem. After drinking tea, he took my hand and spoke to me, then Omar's hand and spoke to him. Papa presented two gold rings on a velvet cushion, which we had to put on each other. Then the imam made a long speech, sitting cross-legged on the couch. He then stood up and came to shake both our hands. He stayed to drink *ahwa*, before congratulating us once more and leaving.

Everyone then pushed their way downstairs and into numerous cars. We took the white Peugeot and drove around the city in convoy, horns blaring out and everyone waving from the windows.

We returned to the flat and the evening passed in a blur. There were so many people, constant music and even a belly-dancer. She had bells around her ankles and wrists and a tiny, glittery costume, which revealed an ample cleavage and a browned, toned midriff. She shook, jangled and bellied her way around the room, paying individual attention to most of the males and making eye contact with them all. She was so brazen, and men and women alike clapped to the rhythm of the dance and egged her on.

There was no alcohol, just some very sweet, sugary syrup, Coke, 7-Up, tea and Turkish coffee, but everyone seemed a little drunk, as if they had been drinking alcohol all night.

Finally, the celebrations drew to a close, the last of the guests left and it was bedtime. I slept with Salma once more, as we had to go through the formal ceremony and be officially man and wife before I could share a bed with Omar. This was planned for the following day.

Lying in bed, reliving the celebrations in my mind, I thought how I was enjoying the idea of being Mrs Omar. It was only then that I realised I had no idea what the surname of the family was. The thought swam round and round in my mind, before I finally gave in to sleep.

'I'm a married woman, and I don't even know my new name.'

13

Loose Ends

The formal registry office ceremony went completely over my head. It was conducted in Arabic from start to finish and I didn't understand a single word.

I was required to repeat garbled nonsense after a very insensitive official. He was aware that I could neither understand nor speak the language, yet made absolutely no allowances for this. He spoke at normal speed, which just sounded like a blur, and expected me to listen and repeat. As his expectations were completely unrealistic, I knew I hadn't a hope of complying. I became flustered and then tearful. This was supposed to be our day and this horrible little man in his brown fez, buck teeth and bad breath was ruining it.

In exasperation, I held up my hands to halt his ranting, and turned away.

'I can't do this,' I told Omar. 'He's spoiling everything. I'm trying really hard, but it's no good, he's not giving me a chance.'

With a roar, Papa was on his feet, shouting at the man, throwing his hands in the air, pointing first at me and then back to the man. Although he towered over Papa, he was soon a quivering wreck, unable to defend himself against such a tirade.

'He is sorry. He will repeat the ceremony for us,' explained Omar.

I turned towards Papa, who flashed me a rare smile.

We resumed our positions and had a rerun, and I repeated his ramblings phrase by phrase. I still didn't understand, but at least I felt as if we were properly married. We signed the register, had it witnessed by Mohamed and Magda, and that was it.

This was day ten, the final day of my holiday. It was obvious, on our return to the flat, that we wouldn't get any time together, just the two of us, so we went for a walk along the river. Hand in hand, husband and wife, we chose a quiet cafe and I listened to the plans Omar was making for us.

'At first, we must live in the flat. Mohamed will move out of my room, so we can have it for ourselves. My father is a builder. He is building a new block of flats and this building will be a lovely one. The first flat to be finished is for Tarek and Mervette. We can have the next one. We will be neighbours.'

'It sounds lovely. How long will it take to finish?'

'Three months, maybe four. Not long.'

I couldn't wait. It was so exciting.

We spent every minute of that day together. Omar was not happy about me flying back to England the following day.

'Cancel the flight. We can arrange another one in a couple of weeks.'

'I can't do that. I need to go back now and explain.'

'If you go now, you will never return to me. I will never see you again.' He turned away.

'Omar, I didn't have to marry you. I could have said no and then none of this would be happening. But I didn't and it is. I love you and I want to spend the rest of my life with you. I can't wait to come back so that we can begin our lives together properly.'

He turned back and I cupped his face in my hands.

'I need to do this, and I need to do it now,' I told him. 'I can't just ignore the pain it would cause my family if I stayed. We cannot simply ride off into the sunset.'

I'm not sure that he understood me completely, but he grasped what I meant and nodded assent.

We had lunch at the Meridian Hotel. I was astonished at the luxury of the place. Huge ornate plates, shiny knives and forks, china cups and saucers, lavish decorations and air-conditioning.

'This is fantastic,' I whispered.

'Why are you whispering?' Omar smiled and I melted.

I gazed at him. I was so happy. I had finally met the man of my dreams. It was just a shame he lived on the other side of the world.

By the time we returned to the flat, Mohamed had moved out of the bedroom and it had been prepared for us. There was a pristine white sheet on the bed, made of beautiful Egyptian cotton, intricately embroidered.

'Look, Omar. It's just right.' I bent down to smell the sheet.

'Crisp and new. Gorgeous, like you. Will anyone disturb us?'

He shook his head, laughing, as we took a flying leap onto the bed. Alone, together at last.

He kissed me deeply, hungrily, letting his hands slide seductively under my blouse. He trailed his fingers from the base of my back up to the nape of my neck and back again. I shivered and reached up to kiss his neck. I moved slowly up to his face, covering it with little kisses and pressing him to me, until our lips met and we kissed more passionately.

He was a gentle, exquisite lover, intent on pleasing me. I had fallen so deeply in love with this man, before making love. Now I was besotted with every part of his body, the smell of his hair and his skin. I wanted to possess and be possessed. I was on fire.

'It's never been like this, ever,' I thought, as we lay spent on the bed.

After showering together, we crept back to our room and lay with our arms wrapped around each other.

'I will love you forever, *habibti*,' he whispered. 'You are my life, my heart and soul. I cannot bear it that you will leave me to go to England.'

'I will be back very soon. Keep the bed warm,' I told him.

Omar sat up, suddenly serious.

'This Dave, you and he, you were his girlfriend?'

'Yes.'

'In England things are different. Did you . . . ?' He trailed off, but I knew what he was asking. I thought for a long while before answering.

'I was with Dave for nearly three years,' I said. 'We would have married one day, but I knew he wasn't the one I wanted to spend the rest of my life with. Yes, we made love. I wanted to end the relationship, but didn't know how to tell him.'

'There has been only Dave?'

'Only Dave.'

I waited while he digested this. Suddenly he was kissing me again.

'Oh Jacky, my love, you are mine now, only mine, forever.'

'. . . and ever.'

I awoke first on that final morning. Omar's arm was draped around me, the other slung out over the end of the bed. His face was relaxed, gentle, innocent. Lightly, I traced the sculptured contours of his face with my finger, before slipping out of bed to shower.

'Jacky, everything is good?'

'Yes, Salma. I am very happy.'

We hugged.

'You make the tea for your husband this morning. I will show you how.'

With a towel wrapped around my head, I followed her into the kitchen, and made the tea. Before lighting the gas, Salma took a cloth and hit the hob several times with it to scare the cockroaches. She managed to step on three, but there were a couple that scuttled away. She then lit the hob and put the kettle on. I found a tray, two glasses, and some sugar for Omar. The milk was in a tin jug. Salma poured tea from a packet into a grey, tin teapot and then I made the tea. There were no strainers, so there were always lots of leaves at the bottom of the glass. A couple of wedges of sponge cake, and I had fulfilled my first duty to be a good Moslem wife.

I could hear Mama in our bedroom, speaking to Omar.

'I wanted to wake him up,' I thought. 'I hope she's not going to interfere now we're married.'

I carried two teas and cake back on a tray. Mama had gone and Omar was sitting in a *galabeya* on a chair.

'Tea and cake brought to you by your wife. Don't expect it every day. Your turn tomorrow,' I joked, although I was half-serious. 'Come back to bed,' I continued, kissing him.

Then I noticed that the sheet had disappeared. The old eiderdown was back in place, with a blanket at the bottom.

'What's happened to the sheet?'

'Mama took it. She has to see the blood.'

'She has to see the what?'

'When a girl marries and sleeps with a man for the first time, there is blood,' explained Omar patiently. 'Mama was making sure it is the first time for you. She wants to see the blood.'

'Oh my God! And what will happen if there is no blood on the sheet?'

I closed my eyes in horror as he replied, 'There can be no marriage and you will be sent away.'

'Well, that's the honeymoon and marriage over in one,' I thought miserably.

'What are we going to do?'

I looked up into his eyes and then buried my face into his chest.

'Well, first we'll eat some cake, and then . . .'

He trailed off. I looked up in surprise to see him smiling broadly.

'Trust me and eat your cake.'

I badgered him for quite some time, but he just kept smiling and wouldn't tell me anything.

A couple of hours later, I was packed and ready to leave. To my surprise, Mama was very cheerful and chatty. I was nearly squeezed to death when she said goodbye. Magda cried and even Papa wiped away a tear.

'*Maasalam, benti.*'

'He says, "Goodbye, my daughter",' Salma translated.

I hugged him.

'*Maasalam, Papa.*'

There were quite a few tears then. Everyone came out into the street to wave me off. Salma was accompanying Omar and me to the airport. Waving until they had completely disappeared, we fell silent. Omar was driving. Salma and I sat quietly, lost in our own thoughts.

My stomach began to tangle up into knots. I slipped my hand into my handbag, feeling the tickets and not one, but two passports tucked away inside. What on earth would I do with Dave's passport and ticket if he didn't turn up? What if something had happened to him? My thoughts ran away with me, leaving me anxious and sweaty.

'He could have been mugged or murdered, and what do I do? Meet someone else and get married. Oh Dave, please be there,' I prayed silently to myself.

I spotted him straightaway, his long hair unmistakable among the Egyptians. Dave's face visibly relaxed as he saw me. He hurried up to us.

'Where the hell did you get to? I've been worried sick. I even went to the police, not that they were bothered. I've been to four hospitals and two youth hostels, but you weren't there.'

He paused for breath, and then looked me up and down.

'Well, you seem okay. Why didn't you get off the bus?' he demanded. 'I couldn't believe it when the bus moved off and you were still on it. I tried to follow . . . And who are these people?'

He looked at Omar and Salma. During his rambling, we had all been standing quietly.

'Dave, I'd like you to meet friends of mine, Omar and his sister, Salma. They have been looking after me. Here, take your ticket and passport and check in, while I say my goodbyes. I'll be with you shortly.'

There was a long, uncomfortable silence. Finally, I thrust the passport at him and turned back to Omar and Salma. They were both fidgety, uncomfortable with the situation. Dave was treating me as an equal and was looking directly into my eyes. By now I had learned enough about the Egyptian culture to know that it was unacceptable for me to speak to another man in such a familiar way. I had to separate them to avoid a scene.

'It's better that you leave now,' I said to Omar. 'I am already upset, and I don't want to cry. I'll be fine.'

I kissed and hugged Salma.

'Thank you for everything.'

I reached up to put my arms round Omar's shoulders. He just buried his face into my neck and held me tightly.

'Remember how much I love you,' I whispered. 'Go, and I'll see you in three weeks. You must trust me. There's only you.'

He was unable to reply. With a slight nod, he turned and left, looking desperately unhappy.

I watched them leave. I felt strangely calm and resolute that what was happening had to happen. At the exit, they turned and raised their hands. I waved back, and walked through to the boarding lounge. It was almost time to board the plane.

14

Goodbyes

'So, what do you have to say for yourself, then?'

We were sitting together on the plane. Dave had settled himself into his seat, and was onto his first drink before he turned his attention to me.

'Well, that's rich, coming from some drunken bum of a boyfriend who was supposed to be looking out for me,' I spat back. 'How dare you, Dave? You were the one who left me to fend for myself on that god-forsaken excuse for a bus.'

'Well, if I remember correctly, it was you who wanted to take the bus, *because it's more authentic.*'

'If you were so concerned, you should have said so at the time.'

'Didn't bother me either way,' he sneered, downing his drink in one.

'Yeah, nothing ever does, does it? Maybe that's the problem.'

'What problem? Have a drink, gal, and it'll all go away.'

'Not this time, Dave.' I waited until he had ordered another drink. 'So tell me what you got up to without me. Did you have a good holiday? Where did you stay?'

'The main youth hostel. There are a few, apparently. Met up

with some blokes from Yorkshire on the first night. Had quite a few good drinking sessions, I can tell you. They left three days ago and I've been looking for you ever since.'

It took a few minutes for all this to sink in.

'So, correct me if I'm wrong. You went on a week-long drinking binge with some mates you hooked up with from Yorkshire. Then, only when they'd left, did you think about looking for me?'

'We didn't just drink. They knew where to get some really great hash. I might have a bit left somewhere.' He started rummaging in his pocket. I could have hit him. 'Nothing. Oh well, I must have smoked the lot.' He altered the seat position to lie back, and closed his eyes.

'So that's it, is it? You're not even going to ask what happened to me?'

'You're going to tell me anyway,' he said.

'Well, before I do, I have something more important to say. It's over between us. It's been over for months. I didn't have the heart to admit it.'

I saw him put down his drink and sit up to listen properly, but I was so angry. I pressed on. 'I only put up with you because we'd booked this holiday. I didn't want to cancel it, so I pretended things were all right between us so I could see Egypt.'

'Oh, charming,' he said.

'Since I've been on holiday, I've met someone who really cares about me, who loves me completely and who would never leave me on a bus on my own. His family loves me too.'

'That's a bit bloody quick,' he said, as if the whole thing was a joke.

'When we get back to England, I'm going to pack my bags and you'll never see me again. But do you know what? This man and his kind family will all see me again, and very soon.' I paused for breath, full of anger and resentment. 'Because I love him with all my heart. And do you know what else I did while I was on this holiday? I went to a wedding.'

Dave took a sip of his drink. 'How interesting for you.'

'Mine.'

As he digested this final piece of information, Dave looked at me in horror.

'You don't believe me, do you? Well, believe this.'

I pulled out the two black-and-white photographs that had been taken of our wedding and thrust them both under his nose. He stared for a long time from one to the other, at me in my beautiful, white wedding gown standing next to Omar in his borrowed, brown velour suit. He didn't say a word. Then he looked at my hand.

'If you're married, where's your wedding ring?'

'We couldn't afford any. We borrowed some for the ceremony. We had to give them back. We will buy some when I go back.'

Dave stared at me. 'You're not joking, are you?'

I shook my head. My anger had disappeared. I wished I hadn't been so angry. He didn't really deserve it.

From that moment, he was quiet and contemplative. He

made no attempt to ask me to change my mind, or ask where we had gone wrong, or if we could try and patch things up. On the coach back home, he sat alone, staring out of the window, stony-faced. I sat several seats behind, quietly crying my eyes out for the hurt I had caused him.

I had a lot to do. I concentrated on the practical aspects, contacting shipping agents, placing advertisements in the paper to sell my things, finding someone to take my place in the house where I rented a room, resigning from my job. I put the two wedding photos into a large envelope with an accompanying letter, and posted them to my parents. Finally, I picked up the telephone and called them.

'Hi, Dad. I'm back. How are you?'

'Hello pet, how nice to hear you. We're both getting along fine.'

'Well, I have some surprising news, and there's no easy way of saying this. Is Mum there?'

'Yes, she's right here. Just a minute. If this is important, you'd better speak to her.'

'Hello, Jacky. How are you, darling? Good holiday?'

'Well, it turned out to be more than just a holiday in the end, Mum.'

'How do you mean, love?'

'You know Dave and I haven't been getting on that well and I've wanted to end everything for quite a while now.'

'Don't tell me, you had a bust-up on holiday.'

'Not exactly, no.'

'Well, what then? Are you still together or not? Spit it out, Jacky.'

I closed my eyes as the words came tumbling out.

'We're not together any more, because we lost each other on the first day, but then I met someone else. Oh Mum, he is so sweet and kind and nice, and I stayed with his family, they're Egyptian by the way, and after a week we fell in love and then he asked me to marry him and of course I said no, but then I thought about never seeing him again, so I said yes, so we got married two days ago and now I'm sorting everything out so I can go back in three weeks and live with him.'

'You did what? Just a minute, hold on there. I have to tell Dad. Are you telling me that you got married and not to Dave?'

'Yes, Mum.'

There was a pause before Dad came on the line. 'Jacky, this is just too much for us to take in. I can't even think about it. I would say things I probably wouldn't mean tomorrow. I'll call you when I've calmed down.'

Click. He rang off. I stared at the receiver. I had forgotten to tell them the photos were in the post.

Two days later, Dad called back.

'Jacky? Come home for Christmas. We received the photos with your letter this morning. We can't accept what you've done. We're shattered and deeply shocked, but we still love you.' He struggled to keep his voice steady. 'So come home as quickly as you can.'

'I'll be with you both as soon as possible. A week should be all I need.'

'We'll talk then.'

'Yes. I love you both. See you soon.'

The line went silent.

I handed in my notice at Kodak, where one of the technicians made another two photos from the wedding negatives before I left. I sold my motorbike to the man who was moving into my room in the house. One week later I was ready to leave.

'Well, this is it. I'm off now.'

'You're still determined to go through with this crazy idea, then?'

'It looks like it, doesn't it?'

Dave had avoided being in the same room as me since we returned. Now he took both of my hands in his.

'You know I still love you.'

'Don't, Dave. It's painful enough as it is. I'm sorry for hurting you, but I have to go.'

I reached up and kissed him on his cheek.

'Happy Christmas.'

He didn't reply.

I arrived home to a barrage of questions from friends and family. Everyone thought I was absolutely crackers. My parents were beside themselves. Christmas preparations were forgotten in the quest to make me see sense and go back to Dave.

'Jacky, what can we do to change your mind?'

'You're making the biggest mistake of your life.'

'I've lost my only daughter.'

'You're an irresponsible, immature girl who needs to grow up.'

Of course, all of these comments immediately forced me onto the defensive, standing up for my love for Omar and my decision to marry him.

On Christmas Eve, I sat in the front room, looking at the Christmas cards placed carelessly on the mantelpiece and bookcases. I could see how the situation was destroying them. Usually Mum loved dressing the house for Christmas, and took great pride in arranging everything creatively to give it the festive feel.

There were pictures of me at various stages of my life dotted all around the house. They were so proud of me, and I was all they had. But if I decided to stay, which was oddly tempting now I was in my comfy English home, I would always wonder what might have been and would never be satisfied with what I had in England.

On Christmas Day, we opened presents and ate a traditional Christmas dinner, but in an emotional, stressful atmosphere. Somehow, it made the food taste awful. Dad poured himself a second brandy, which I had never seen him do before.

'Mum and Dad, I can feel the pain you are feeling. I don't expect you to condone any of this, but if you would try and accept the situation at least, it would be easier for you to bear.'

'We will always worry about you, never mind running off with some foreigner. Please tell us it's not happening, Jacky. Your dad's heartbroken.'

'Mum, I love Omar very much and I want to be where he is. I need to do this and follow my heart. He has made me so happy.'

'So far maybe,' Dad interrupted, 'but what happens when that first flush of love begins to fade? What will you be left with then? A bloody nightmare, I can tell you. You're making a big mistake, Jacky. You've always been headstrong and determined; qualities your mum and I both admired you for, but this . . .'

His voice broke and he held his head in his hands, unable to continue. Eventually he whispered, 'Your mum and I will always love you.'

'I love you too, and hate what this is doing to you. I'm so sorry to make you suffer. I'm sure we will be able to visit, and you can come over to see us. Who knows? We may even think of settling here in England.'

Mum burst into tears. 'Oh Jacky, please don't leave us. Have second thoughts, darling. There must be a way round all this.'

She hugged me, and I saw that Dad had turned his face away, but his body was shaking with sobs.

'Our lives will be empty without you,' he cried. He blew his nose forcefully into his handkerchief.

'Oh Dad, please don't cry. I'll write all the time. We can phone each other. It'll be as if I'm still working for Kodak. The only difference will be the distance.'

'The only difference,' he mumbled, unconvinced.

It was pointless trying to reassure them, I realised. Just as it was pointless in the end them trying to persuade me to stay.

One week later, I hugged them both goodbye at the airport.

'I will make this work. You'll see. I'll make you proud of me,' I assured them, kissing them for the last time.

As I turned to wheel the trolley away, my mother stifled a sob and I heard her whisper, 'But we're already proud of you.'

I looked back at my parents. They had always been happy together, from the day they first met. All I wanted was to build the same sort of life with Omar. They didn't know how much I admired them and trusted their opinions, probably more than I even realised myself.

The flight to Cairo was being called. I turned away. An adventure was about to begin and, after all the tears, deep down, I was happy and excited.

15

Down to Earth

'Excuse me, *shokran, shokran,* thank you.'
I jostled my way to the front of the plane, making good use of the only Arabic word I had learnt so far to make my way to the exit more quickly.

As the plane touched down at Cairo airport and it was finally time to get off, a sense of urgency rushed through me. I was bursting to see Omar again, to actually be with him for days, weeks and months. I tried to picture his face in my mind, but the details were fuzzy.

'I can't remember his face. The eyes are still there, but I can't picture his whole face.'

As I stumbled from the metal stairway into the airport building, urgency was suddenly replaced by apprehension, even fear. My confidence took an almighty dive. What if he'd forgotten the features of my face? What if he'd forgotten our promises? Would he be there to meet me? Had he changed his mind about us?

I passed through passport control and on to the luggage carousel in a daze. I began to wonder why on earth I hadn't considered this before. It was New Year's Eve and I'd been away for three weeks. We had only known each other for two. Maybe he'd had time to consider the enormity of what we'd done and had decided he didn't want me any more.

With three large suitcases and my hand luggage piled on a trolley, the customs officer waved me by without any questions. As I pushed my way through the crowds, I was already forming a plan of action.

'Right. If there's no one here to meet me, I'll wait for half an hour, put this lot in left luggage and try to arrange a flight home. And this time, I'll stay there.'

'Jacky, Jacky, over here.'

'Jacky, *habibti, marati*, welcome.'

I looked up, puzzled. The whole family were at the end of the building, behind the wire barriers, waving and shouting. Immediately I could see Omar's smiling face, his beautiful brown eyes, his features instantly clear again in my mind. I rushed towards him and buried my face in his hair, and whispered loving words into his ear, breathing in the familiar smell of his clothes mingled with Paco Rabanne.

Mama pulled me roughly towards her, smothering me with kisses. We all piled into the white Peugeot, everyone shouting at the same time. I sat on Omar's knee, my arm around his neck, smiling and nodding at everyone, caught up in their enthusiasm.

'This is it. I'm here. This is my home now,' I thought.

Looking out of the window, I watched two women in black *millaya* walking barefoot, carrying huge gas bottles on their heads. Others were sitting by the roadside, selling vegetables.

Some were sitting in the dust, chatting and breastfeeding babies. One boy, about three years old, lay across his mother sucking at one breast while she nursed a baby at the other. It was strange, I thought, that these women, who are required to cover themselves from head to toe in black, bare their breasts to feed their young in public without a care in the world.

I turned my attention back to the babble in the car, but could not make head or tail of any of it. I smiled and squeezed Omar's hand. I was dying to kiss him, but I'd have to wait until we were alone. I stared out of the window again, this time deep in thought. If we had been in England, I would have been kissing him right there in the car, but I was in Egypt now. I had to respect their customs and try to be like them.

'Life can't possibly be all that different, once I get used to it.'

I couldn't have been more wrong.

My 'homecoming' made me feel warm, welcome and wanted. The family was obviously delighted and excited to see me again, and upon our arrival at the flat, showered me with attention, bringing me 7-Up and cake, hugging and kissing me, badgering Salma to ask me question after question, never waiting for an answer of course. Even the television was switched off – a real honour.

When the call to prayer interrupted our gaiety, most of the family began preparing to pray and then have a siesta. Omar and I could be alone together at last.

The front bedroom had been prepared for us, which meant that Mohamed was relegated to the spare bed in Salma's room.

There was a *galabeya* laid out for me to wear. Apart from Papa, who generally wore thick, cotton, stripy pyjamas, the rest of the family wore *galabeyas* whenever they were in the house.

'I suppose it's because of the heat,' I mused, as I fingered the pretty embroidery around the neck. It was a beautiful shade of pale blue, almost like the sky on a clear day, with delicate white stitching around the neck and sleeves. Men wore only white, yet women could be as bold as they liked when it came to choosing the colours they wore in the home.

Omar suddenly appeared, his prayers over. His arms were around me and he was kissing me, stroking my hair, burying his face in my neck and all the while talking quietly yet urgently. I was in heaven. He was the most gorgeous man I'd ever laid eyes on, and here he was, telling me he loved me, peeling off the *galabeya*, making love to me. Sex wasn't good, it was unbelievable. We seemed to be made for each other.

'Come, we must shower.'

'You go. I'm feeling lazy. I'll go later.'

'No, my darling. We must. In the Koran, it is written that we must wash immediately after we make love. We must both shower now and be clean.'

'Oh, I didn't realise. Sorry.'

'We'll go together, but we must be very quiet.'

Wrapped in towels, we crept along the dark corridor to the bathroom at the end, and quickly closed the door behind us. The cold water startled me as it gushed over us. Omar took the soap and began to wash me with sweeping movements up and down my skin. I shivered, and reached up to kiss him, taking the soap to wash him at the same time.

We were soon back in our room, where he reached for a cigarette, the local brand, Cleopatra. I snuggled back under the bedspread, almost bursting with happiness.

'I've truly found my soul mate,' I thought to myself. 'I'm so totally in love with you and completely in lust with you. You give me butterflies in my stomach just thinking about you.'

That first evening, aunts, uncles and cousins visited, eager to welcome me into the family. They were all so happy to see me, each one trying to sit next to me and teach me this or that word in Arabic. Magda put on some Arabian music, and people began to clap rhythmically, as one by one the wives and girls tied a cotton belt around their hips and began to dance, swinging their hips around and wriggling their bellies. They held out their arms and twisted their hands up and out, sometimes even leaning forward and shaking their breasts to the music. I was fascinated, but not willing to give it a try when they asked me.

The evening drew to a close at midnight. It had been a great success. I had genuinely enjoyed myself, and was grateful for such a warm welcome.

Back in our room together, Omar and I slipped under the bedspread. There were no sheets now.

'So what will you do tomorrow? What do I do now that I am your wife?'

'Tomorrow? I go to the university to study. Then I go to my father's workshop to earn some money. You will stay with

Mama and help her. When I return we will walk together up to the bridge and have a drink.'

He kissed me gently, reassuringly. 'Don't look so worried, *habibti*. We have each other now. It is all I want, to come home to my lovely wife, *marati*, each night. You will be fine in the flat with Mama.'

'And so my new life begins,' I thought. I lay there listening to the constant noise of the traffic outside as Omar slept peacefully, his arms wrapped tightly around me.

16

Teething Problems

Although the family made me welcome, I was expected automatically to adapt to their ways, with absolutely no compromise. At first it wasn't a problem, as I was so eager to learn and prove to everyone, including myself, that I could do it. I was desperate to fit in.

It transpired that all the excursions I had been on with the family previously were not the norm at all. In fact, Salma and Magda had not even been to most of the places before. A day trip was a rare occurrence for them, being girls, which explained their enthusiasm when we had gone out together. Their daily routine was far more mundane. If they hadn't needed to go to school or university, they could have stayed within the walls of that flat for weeks.

It gradually became clear that if anything was needed and there was a male hanging around, then he popped out to get it, leaving the women mostly indoors. As the flat was virtually on the ground floor, the windows opened out onto the main street just above people's heads as they passed by. Sunbathing was out of the question. They hated the sun anyway and the shutters were permanently either completely shut or a tad ajar, letting the tiniest shaft of sunlight through. So the days were literally gloomy.

As an Egyptian wife, I was expected to do my share. Washing the floor was an experience; dirty bits of an old sack soaked in a bowl of water and 'walked' around the floor with our feet. Then we 'squidgied' up the excess with a rubber blade that I'd only ever used for windows. This one was the size of a broom with a long handle on it. Finally a dry sack was 'walked' over the floor to dry it off. Dirty water was swilled down a drain under the shower on the bathroom floor.

The bathroom contained a bath, a sink, a toilet and a shower. The sink was a normal sink, where the family washed their feet before praying. The bath was a washing machine in disguise. It was only used to soak and wash sheets and towels and no one ever took a bath.

One particularly hot, sticky day, I tentatively approached Salma and broached this sensitive subject.

'Salma, do you think it would be possible for me to have a bath today?'

'Jacky, of course. Why do you ask? You may shower at any time.'

'Thank you, but I didn't mean a shower. I meant a bath.'

There was a short silence, as Salma digested this. She then grabbed my hand and dragged me into Papa's room, where he was watching TV with Mama and Magda.

'Jacky has just asked me if she can have a bath. She wants to use the bath to sit in and wash herself. Can you believe it?'

The television was temporarily forgotten as they fell about

laughing. Magda held her sides and shrieked with laughter, Mama howled, leaning against Papa, who looked at me, chuckling delightedly.

'Don't bother with the comedy programme,' I thought. 'You've got your own personal comedienne right here. All I have to do is ask for a bath and you're hysterical.'

'Why would you want to sit in your dirty water, when you can have a shower and be very clean?' Salma walked away, still smiling to herself.

Of course, it was a ludicrous suggestion. Fancy thinking that the bath was there in order to have a bath. You really must try to be more discerning, I told myself, as I returned to the bathroom to take a shower.

The shower was at the back of the bathroom, with a large tap at the base. There was no cubicle, door or curtain of any kind, just a drain beneath. This meant that every time someone took a shower, the floor was completely soaked. It was cold water; there was no hot. The men used the bathroom and left it awash; the women were expected to 'squidgy' and wipe up after them. Two smelly sacks were slung over a line above the bath for this purpose, causing a dank, wet-sack smell all the time.

The toilet was white, ceramic and modern. There was no seat, but far, far better than other alternatives I had seen: a hole in the middle of a tiled square with two raised sections either side for the feet. This was ultimately impractical and utterly unmanageable.

Protruding into the toilet bowl was a thin, metal tube

connected to a tap on the wall. This enabled a jet of water to enter the bowl and you could clean yourself that way – with your left hand – when you had finished. The family maintained that we Europeans were a dirty race, wiping our bottoms with paper. They considered themselves far more hygienic, using running water.

By far the most important chore of the day for women was the preparation of the food. This was a massive job and could take hours to complete.

It involved one of the girls leaving the house to buy fresh vegetables from the *souk*. If they were buying provisions from the little local shops, they dressed carefully, doing their hair and applying make-up. However, if they were visiting the *souk*, then they flung a black robe over themselves and covered their hair with a flowery scarf. This made them look like the very poor, whom they called *baladi*, and in this way they could haggle and buy the vegetables at a much better price.

The food was always covered in dust and had to be rinsed again and again. Then there was the peeling or the chopping of the various vegetables, or the folding of the cabbage leaves. Vegetables were never simply boiled. They were always flavoured with tomato puree, lemon juice and garlic. We coated cauliflower florets in batter and deep-fried them.

This was all strange to me, and the end result was not at all appealing. I couldn't seem to get used to the basic taste of the food. One particular vegetable, supposed to be a favourite of most Egyptians, consisted of green leaves, which they called *mollogheya*. After copious rinsing, it was turned out onto a chopping board where it was ground into a sticky, mushy substance using a two-handled blade, which was rocked from side to side. It took absolutely ages to produce this gooey mess. When I tried, my wrists felt as if they were about to break by the time Mama was satisfied that it was ready. The *mollogheya* is then cooked in a pan with garlic and water, to make slimy green soup. It can be eaten with rice, or simply scooped up into pieces of *ayish*, or bread.

By far the worst job in the kitchen was cleaning the rice. No easy-cook, bagged-up, off-the-shelf rice. Oh, no. The rice came in sacks, along with countless tiny stones and husks. Every day, we had to pour the required amount into a large flour sieve and sort through, grain by grain, with our fingers, discarding all the stones, husks and dead insects. This took at least an hour, and then it had to be rinsed until the water ran clear – usually about ten or twelve rinses. Only then was it ready to be cooked. It was a tiresome, tedious, thankless task that I dreaded.

The preparation of food would at least have been something to break up the long days. It was a shame that I was finding it hard to get used to the taste of their cuisine.

Omar left us to it during the day, obviously happy that I was being taken under the family's wing. He was so busy himself, rushing from lectures to the workshop. He was studying librarianship. Knowing that he was intent on joining the family business after gaining his degree, I did wonder what use this would be to him in the future. I'm not sure why, probably just because wives did not question their husbands, but I never got around to asking him about it. There were no such things as educational grants in Egypt, which meant that we were dependent on the family until he finished his studies and began earning a proper wage.

The novelty of our daily routine wore off very quickly, and I began to miss Omar terribly. We were never alone.

'How long will it be before we can move into our flat, Omar? Can we go and see it? Is it very far away?'

I pressed him continually for answers, needing to hear that we would soon be moving to a place of our own, until one day, he came in smiling, took my hands in his and slipped a tiny box into them.

'I have been working hard for these. Try yours and then get changed. I want to take you to see our flat.'

Slowly I opened the dark red box. Nestling inside were two wedding rings.

'They're beautiful. Mine's a perfect fit. Try yours.'

'I already did. It fits, but I wanted us to put them on together.'

I slipped his ring onto his finger, as he did the same to me. Five minutes later, I had changed and we were driving out to see our flat in Embaba.

'When we live here, if you go out, you must cover your hair with a scarf. Many of these people have never seen someone with blonde hair. Here. Put this on.'

He handed me a black scarf, which I wrapped around my head and neck, covering every inch of my blonde hair.

The road was not smooth tarmac like the road outside Papa's flat. It was bumpy, dusty and full of carts pulled by donkeys, poor thin creatures that were regularly whipped by the drivers. Eventually, we turned off this makeshift road onto a side road that was more like a dirt track, with makeshift houses and crude blocks of flats with peeling paint and missing bricks. So this was Embaba and certainly the poorest part of Cairo I'd seen so far.

Children in pyjamas were running around barefoot. They looked grubby, with stained yellow teeth; many had flies crawling over their faces and into their eyes, which they didn't bother to wipe away. They all stopped to watch us drive into their street and park to one side. As we got out, they surrounded the car, interested in anything different that happened during their day.

To my surprise, instead of smiling and chatting to them, Omar's face darkened, and he bellowed at them to go away, actually pushing one boy to the floor. They all shrank away to the other side of the street, some disappearing into the dark recesses of the buildings to peer out from the safety inside.

'Come, up here.' Omar spoke in English. He directed me up a flight of dusty steps.

'Why did you shout at them? They are only children. They weren't harming anyone.'

Omar, in front of me, stopped and turned to face me.

'Jacky, you know nothing about these people. They are nothing. They need to respect me and listen to me. I know what I am doing and how to speak to these people. Do not question me again.'

I looked up at him to laugh, but the smile drained away as I took in his expression. His face was deadly serious.

We climbed up to the fourth floor. There were two doors on either side of the stairs.

'That will be for Tarek and Mervette,' Omar explained, 'and this one will be ours,' he continued, turning the key in the lock and opening the door.

I had been instantly subdued at his reaction to the children, but on entering the flat the feeling disappeared as I looked around.

The door opened straight into a large area with a smaller recess at the back – the living area, or reception hall as Omar called it. Two doors on the left revealed two bedrooms, the smaller of the two having a tiny balcony. Bricks, planks of wood, shutters and stones were piled everywhere and none of the windows had been fitted.

In actual fact, it was dusty, filthy and unbearably hot, but I didn't notice any of this. Already I was picturing us living there, in our own place, just the two of us together. I was excited to see our future home for real, rather than have to sit at Papa's house and just imagine what it would be like, and was suddenly filled with renewed hope for the future.

'Omar, it's wonderful. Bigger than I had imagined. What's through there?'

There was a tiny corridor at the far corner of the living area. It led to a small bathroom on the right and a room on the left.

'This will be the kitchen. Downstairs Papa has made a small workshop, where his men will make kitchen cupboards for the flats. But we must save up for a fridge and a cooker.'

I nodded and looked round the little bathroom. A sink, toilet and shower, with a window opening out to the centre of the building.

'If you want, I can put a bath in for you, under the shower.'

'Yes, I'd love that. Thank you.' I reached up and kissed him. 'When do you think it will be ready?'

'Soon, *habibti*, soon.'

I turned and ran into the second bedroom to stand on the little balcony.

'Get inside, now,' he shouted.

In an instant he was beside me. He took hold of my arm roughly and dragged me back.

'Do you want the whole world to see you? Do you want them to know our business? You must not show yourself like this.'

He grabbed the black scarf, which I had taken off and was holding, and flung it at me. It fell to the floor. Slowly I bent down to retrieve it. When I looked up at his face, full of anger, watching me, I suddenly changed my mind and left it where it was.

'Look, this is stupid. We're here in our future home, and you tell me to wear that?' I pointed at the scarf on the floor. 'For one thing, it's far too hot, and for another, so what if the neighbours see me? They're only the neighbours. So get off your high horse, calm down, and let's enjoy looking round.'

I turned away from him, left the scarf where he had thrown it and went through into the other bedroom.

'Come, Jacky. We must go now.'

He was standing in the doorway.

'But I'm not ready yet.'

'We go now.'

The journey back to the house was tense. Not a word was spoken.

'I've really upset him. I should try harder. All I had to do was to put on that stupid scarf. Why did I have to argue? I've just spoilt everything now.'

He dropped me off, but didn't come in. I heard the tyres screech as he headed off up the street. He didn't even say goodbye. I fled to our room and threw myself sobbing on the bed.

Much later, Omar crept into the room and wrapped his arms around me. 'Jacky, Jacky, I love you with all my heart. Why do you fight me?'

With a sob, I leant against him. 'Will you forgive me? I didn't mean to make you so angry. I'll try harder to be a good wife. I'm sorry.'

That night when we made love, I was far more passive than I had been before. I let Omar make love to me. Conflicting emotions were running through my head: love for him, guilt for making him angry, anger for my lack of tact, regret that we'd had our first argument so early in the marriage. After showering, Omar lay beside me smoking. He was happy again.

'You know, darling, I feel so good. It was the best it has ever been for me. You are so very beautiful.'

As he slept, I lay awake, thinking about the events of the day.

'You are going to have to try much harder,' I told myself. 'And you must remember not to be so dominant in bed.'

17

Back to School

Life quickly formed a routine, so unchanging that the days merged into one another. I did make a great effort to learn Arabic, writing down new words daily and poring over them at every opportunity. The alphabet was totally different and I wrote down the words phonetically, according to how they were said. This helped with my pronunciation, and after only a short time I was building small sentences and questions, and using them whenever I could.

This pleased the rest of the family. They were becoming interested in English and I began to teach them as they taught me. I often helped Salma with her homework and she showed me books on the Arabic alphabet. It baffled me. Arabic is written from right to left. Then each letter is written differently depending on whether it is at the beginning, middle or end of a word. To cap it all, the language written in books and newspapers is classical Arabic, which is totally different from the colloquial Arabic spoken in the street. So even if I managed to decipher the letters of a word in a newspaper, I still didn't have a clue what it meant.

* * *

About a month after we had gone to see the flat, Omar came into our room, where I was sitting writing a letter home.

'Jacky? What are you doing? Why do you not sit with the family and watch the *tamsalaya*?'

'I'm just writing a letter home. I feel really tired. I learnt how to cook *koshari* today. Then I washed all the floors by myself and my back is killing me.'

'Do you mind if I go and watch it?'

''Course not. I'll come and join you when I've finished.'

I sighed. I felt weary. Weary of getting through each day with nothing of interest to tell Omar when he came in. It hadn't taken long for the boredom to set in, and I was becoming boring with it. I needed to fill my life with something more than household chores. And then it hit me. I smiled to myself as I slipped quietly into the back bedroom and whispered for Omar to come out.

'Can we go for a walk? I feel like some fresh air and a chat.'

Sitting on the wall by the river, we ate corn and drank Coke.

'How's the work on the flat going? Are the windows in yet?'

'Not yet, but they will be - soon.'

'You work such long hours, and we hardly see each other. When we do, you're so tired.'

'But we need all the money I can earn. I'm doing it for us. One day we will have everything we need.'

'So what would you say if I found a job to help out? I could teach English, in an English school, or privately. Is it forbidden for Egyptian wives to work?'

At this, Omar looked up sharply, obviously surprised at my suggestion. I took a deep breath and continued.

'Of course, if it is frowned upon, then I won't mention it again. I want to be a good wife to you.'

As I said this, his face visibly relaxed. He thought for a moment before giving his reply.

'You are the best wife in the world. Yes, it is a good idea. I will ask my friend Hesham about this. He knows someone whose son attends an English school.'

I hugged him delightedly.

'Not bad, not bad at all,' I congratulated myself. 'Just let him think he is in control and I can have what I want.'

The following day, after university, Omar collected me and we went to see Hesham. It was good to see him again. Had it only been a couple of months ago that he had helped me from the street with Omar? It seemed more like years. He ushered us into the reception hall of his home. He was delighted to see us, shaking my hand and saying, *'Mabrouk'*.

I smiled back at him. *'Shokran, Hesham.'*

When his mother appeared, her head covered with a veil, I stood up to greet her, saying, *'Ahlan, ahlan, ezayik.'*

Her face lit up as she returned the greeting and proceeded to bring tea, cakes and sweets. She sat close to me, and kept taking hold of my cheek to say, *'Eshta'* or *'Lateefa'*, and smiling broadly, revealing three gold teeth.

When she left us to talk, Hesham told me that these were compliments; she had called me pretty and likened me to cream, which is another way of saying she liked me. I drank the black, sweet tea without complaint, as the two men discussed my idea.

'Hesham will come with us to the school and introduce you. The headmistress there is English. Okay, darling?'

'Of course. When shall we go?'

'Now.'

We left Hesham's mother, who kissed me fiercely on both cheeks and squeezed my arm tightly. Her skin was wrinkled and dry and she smelt faintly of garlic. She was little more than forty but looked worn out.

'*Maasalam benti, maasalam.*'

The school was situated in an old villa. I don't know what I was expecting, but it wasn't that. The headmistress was happy to meet me. After a short introduction by Hesham, she shook hands with Omar and we went to sit in her office.

'So, how long have you been in Cairo?'

I looked up, surprised. It had been a long time since I had had a conversation with another English person and I relaxed as the conversation flowed naturally and easily.

Mrs Sellar and her husband George had lived in Cairo for five years and had come to the city to be close to their daughter, who had married an Egyptian. They had bought the villa and opened the school after a year. The children who attended were mainly from rich Egyptian families. Egyptian teachers taught environmental studies, geography, history and *deen* (religion), in Arabic. The English staff taught English, maths and science in English.

During our tour of the school, I explained to Omar what had been said. When she heard us conversing in French, she turned abruptly.

'Ah, I see you speak French. I have a vacancy for a teacher, and if you accept I would love it if you would also teach French.'

We returned to her office where she arranged for coffee to be brought. She smiled at my reaction to a mug of white, unsweetened coffee.

'Nescafé from England. We have another daughter at home who sends things like Marmite and gravy granules. I guessed you'd like a mug of instant coffee.'

'If only you knew how much.'

I hadn't been particularly keen on coffee back in England, but in that moment, the mere aroma awoke my taste buds, and to actually taste unsweetened coffee was sheer heaven.

After further discussion about pay and hours, Mrs Sellar formally offered me a job, which Omar was happy for me to accept. I was required to attend a briefing the following day. Luckily the school bus passed by the flat.

There was a downside concerning the pay. Had I been the wife of an Englishman who was working for a company in Cairo, I would have been paid 300LE per month. As the wife of an Egyptian national, I would earn only 54LE. Such was the status of women in Egypt, and it made me wonder how we would manage on such a wage when we eventually moved out of Papa's flat.

* * *

The following day, I waited for the minibus to arrive. Mr Sellar was driving. Magda came out to wave goodbye, and Mama flung open the green shutters to see me off. There were several children already on the bus, and they giggled and pointed at me. I turned to smile at them.

'Good morning, children. Morning, Mr Sellar.'

'Morning. Call me George, everyone else does.' He smiled at me and cocked his head towards the children. 'They are too shy to talk to you, but they are lovely kids once you get to know them.'

He stopped several more times to pick up groups of children, who all stared unblinkingly at me as they passed by to find a seat. I noticed that they were very different from the children I had seen in Egypt so far. They carried smart school bags and lunchboxes. Their fingernails were clean and they smelt of soap and shampoo. The girls' hair was brushed, carefully styled and decorated with clips and ribbons. Probably their most striking feature was their teeth, which they revealed constantly, giggling at me. They all had two rows of brilliant white, shining teeth, in such stark contrast to the children in Embaba, or on the streets and in the *souk*. My mind flashed back to the image of those poor, ragged children who had excitedly crowded around the car. I remembered the face of the little boy who Omar had roughly pushed to the ground. He had already lost some of his teeth.

When we arrived at the school, the children rushed out of the minibus and went with two Egyptian women wearing white overalls and white veils to put away their lunchboxes and bags.

Then they went out to play before the start of lessons. George took me into the briefing, where I met the other teachers.

There were five British girls. Judith and Lisa were married to Englishmen who had come out to Cairo on contract with Rothmans. As we chatted it became obvious that they were very well off and lived in luxury apartments in Zamalek, a very affluent area of the city. They each had two company cars and could afford to shop at the supermarkets. It was ironic that they earned so much more than I would, and didn't really need it, and I was desperate to earn money and was offered a pittance.

We hit it off instantly and I was as intrigued by their lifestyle in Cairo as they were in mine. The other three girls, Christine, Karen and Elizabeth, were all, like me, married to Egyptian men. We didn't get the chance to chat that first day, as Mrs Sellar came in and the briefing began.

Teaching was a new experience and I threw myself into it. The children were friendly and enthusiastic, and the mere fact that I could have a proper conversation and a giggle in my own language was like a breath of fresh air. I hadn't missed this before now, but realised how much more fulfilled my life was going to be. My spirits lifted as the day wore on, and when George dropped me off at four o'clock, I fairly ran up the steps to tell the family all about it.

I had to ring and ring the doorbell, until at last a sleepy Mohamed opened the door and let me in. The flat was in darkness. It was siesta time. I tiptoed into the kitchen to make tea and carried it back to our room, where Omar was resting. I shook him gently, bending to nuzzle his neck and stroke his hair.

'I'm back. Tea?'

He stirred and sat up smiling, pulling me to him and kissing me. 'Do you like your job? It is very good if my wife works in an English school.' He got up to look at himself in the mirror. 'People will look up to us.'

I got up to pass him his tea. I had been bursting to tell him every detail, but now it was clear that he wasn't bothered about details.

'Yes, I like the job. It's fine. Drink your tea.'

'There is still the food to prepare for us. Mama said she would not do it. You must continue to be a good wife, even if you work,' he said abruptly and got up to take a shower.

I wandered into the kitchen to make a start on the tedious task of sorting, cleaning and rinsing rice. My back was aching and I felt so tired. As I threw out the tiny grey stones, my mind drifted back to the events of the day and I brightened up instantly. I could see a rosy future ahead, with me teaching, and Omar and I living in our own place.

Omar stuck his head into the kitchen. 'After we eat, I'll take you out tonight. We can walk up to the second bridge.'

As I got to grips with my work duties and began building relationships with the other girls there, life with Mama was more bearable. I became more content and confident, and Omar and I hardly had a cross word between us. The only thing to spoil these first weeks was my continual backache, headache and general tiredness. Some days after school, I would have to drag myself up the few stairs to the flat. Finally I came in one afternoon and collapsed on the bed. When Omar woke me, I just burst into tears.

'Oh Omar, I feel terrible. I'm so tired and my back aches. It just never stops.'

'Come, darling, Mama will make you some tea. You'll feel better after a rest. I need to go out to fetch something. I will be back before you have finished your tea.'

I nodded miserably. 'I'm sorry for being such a nuisance.'

He hugged me. 'Oh no, my darling. You are wonderful.'

As he left, and Mama appeared with tea, I wondered what he had meant, and why Mama had such a beaming smile when she left me to drink it. Omar returned shortly afterwards, a paper bag in his hand.

'Here you are. This will make sure.'

Inside the bag was a home pregnancy test kit. I stared from it to him and back again. Slowly, things began to fall into place.

'You mean, the backache, the tiredness?' I stopped to think. 'Oh my God!'

He laughed and pulled me off the bed, twirling me around. 'Yes, my beautiful darling wife. You're going to have a baby. Our baby.'

I was in shock. 'But how did you know?'

'Mama knows these things,' he said, tapping the side of his nose. 'Do the test, so you believe her.'

I read the side of the box.

'I need to wait until the morning. I'll wake you up and tell you before I go to school.'

'You don't need to tell me anything.' Omar kissed me for a long time before whispering, 'I already know.'

All night I lay in bed, unable to sleep, mulling it over. Me, pregnant? I was barely married. I was still trying to adapt to a brand new life and take care of myself. Was I ready to look after someone else? The question scared me. I let my hands trail over my stomach. I didn't feel pregnant. I only had backache and the odd headache, that was all. There again, I didn't know what being pregnant felt like.

My hands moved upwards from my stomach onto each breast. I stroked them gently and was surprised at how tender they were. Was this another symptom of pregnancy, or was there something really seriously wrong with me? I had no idea.

After a fitful night, I got up at six o'clock, and did the test in the bathroom. I showered while waiting for something to happen in the little window of the white plastic container. I didn't bother to wake Omar. I made tea for myself, dressed and sat quietly waiting for George to pick me up. I threw myself into teaching, and it was only when I took a break at lunchtime that I allowed myself to think about Omar.

He was going to be surprised that I had not bothered to wake him. He would be annoyed that I had not made him any tea. But I had absolutely no idea how he would feel when he looked on the chair beside the bed where I had left the plastic container with the clear blue line telling him that he was definitely going to be a father.

18

The Joys of Pregnancy

'Congratulations, Jacky. Well done!'

'You certainly didn't waste any time.'

'Make the most of the next nine months – you'll certainly have your hands full after that.'

'My first was the worst, screaming every night for six months, but I'm sure you'll be fine.'

The girls at school were all excited to hear my news. It triggered off many of their own experiences of pregnancy, birth and motherhood, all of which they related in great detail and some of which I could have done with not hearing at all.

'So, how do you feel about becoming a mum?' asked Elizabeth.

'Frightened to death. I haven't a clue what to do with babies. I could make a mistake and drop it or something.' I put my head in my hands.

'That's okay. Every woman feels like that, don't they, girls?' said Christine. She looked around and all the English mums nodded their heads in agreement.

'I never felt like that,' Aisha, an Egyptian teacher, remarked. 'In our family, we are expected to marry and have children. So when I became pregnant for the first time, I was happy and excited, because my family were there to help.'

'My family will be there for me too,' I replied. 'My husband's thrilled. But I just can't get rid of this knotted-up feeling inside. I had never even dreamed of having babies.'

Aisha looked shocked. 'Oh, but if you marry an Egyptian man, you must have babies.'

'I know. It's just that I hadn't even got used to the idea of being married. Everything is happening so quickly,' I replied.

'This is not quick, this is normal,' Aisha said with a smile, and leant forward to pat my shoulder. 'You have done well, Jacky. Your family will be proud of you.'

The only contact I'd had with my family in England was by letter. There was a telephone in the house but, as we were not contributing to the household finances, I felt embarrassed to ask to make an international call. So I wrote to tell my parents the news. It was a chatty, newsy letter, as I really hadn't a clue how to express myself. I wasn't that pleased about being pregnant, and to write the truth would only worry them all the more.

Two weeks later, there was a phone call from them.

'Jacky?'

'Hello, Mum.' At the sound of her voice, I burst into tears, holding the receiver away from me so that she wouldn't hear me.

'Your Dad and I just want you to know how pleased we are for you. Congratulations, darling. You'll make a wonderful mum.'

'Thank you,' was all I managed to blurt out.

'How are you? Is life treating you well? Are you happy?'

'Very happy, Mum. Everything's even better than I thought it was going to be. How are you both?'

'Fine, darling. We're just so pleased to hear your voice. Your father's a little emotional at the moment. We both miss you.'

'I miss you too. When we have our own flat, I'll save up and phone you regularly, Mum.'

'Okay, darling. Must go now, we'll phone again in a couple of weeks. We love you.'

As I replaced the receiver, I felt calmer about things. What fantastic parents I had. I knew Mum had been dying to ask about hospitals, conditions, giving birth, the reaction of the family here and all about my relationship with Omar. Yet she had brushed aside her need for reassurance to give me her blessing. She had put my feelings before hers.

Strangely, I had reassured her that things were going well, even though my life was a continual struggle, which filled me with self-doubt whenever I slipped up.

The following day, Karen was absent from school.

'She will be in tomorrow, she has a migraine,' Mrs Sellar informed us during the briefing.

Judith leaned over to me and whispered, 'And we all know what that means.'

I had no idea what she was talking about.

Now I had the approval of my parents, my initial worries faded and I became more excited about having a baby. It was only when I started to write a long, detailed letter to Mum about hospitals and giving birth in Cairo, that I realised how little I knew. I wanted to know so many things, and the girls at school were the ones who could help me.

'Elizabeth, is there a national health service?'

Six of us were sitting outside in the shade on rickety chairs with flaky, white paint. No one ever sat on the ground. It was far too dusty with insects running all over. The children were watching a video indoors, and we had a rare hour and a half to relax.

'Oh yes, and everyone gets a huge pension at forty.'

I looked up in surprise. Her face was deadly serious, but then Aisha burst out laughing and the others followed suit.

'Of course there's no national health here. The only thing around here that could be remotely referred to as "national" is the army.'

'So how do I have a baby, then?' I asked.

'Well, you wait for the pains, you open your legs . . .' Christine stopped, unable to carry on without giggling.

'You know what I mean. What happens exactly? Do I go to see a doctor? Do I give birth in a hospital or at home?'

One of the other Egyptian teachers, a quiet, attractive girl called Leila, answered. 'Your husband should organise a doctor and a hospital for you, or you can have the baby at home. It is a wonderful occasion. Ask your husband. He will be happy to arrange things just as you want them.'

Suddenly I was full of hope.

'Thank you, Leila. I'll do that. Oh, it's great being pregnant.'

That evening, I asked Omar everything. I was so impatient to hear the answers that each question tumbled out after the other, giving him no time to answer any one of them. He eventually gave up trying and began to laugh.

'*Habibti marati, shwiya, shwiya, kalimni shwiya.*'

'Do I need to see a doctor?'

'Not yet. Mama will know if there is anything wrong, so there is no need. We have no money for a doctor. Every visit will cost money. Don't worry, everything will be fine.'

Two weeks later I awoke feeling dreadful. Nausea swept over me in waves. Shakily, I made my way to the bathroom, but was hit by the awful odours wafting out from the kitchen on the way. Hints of tomato and garlic mingled with stale cigarettes, and the stench from the damp sacking made me retch.

I dragged myself to school, knowing it must be morning sickness. My aim was to survive until noon. Lunchtime came but the sickness showed no signs of abating. I couldn't face any lunch. My sense of smell was heightened to such a degree that I was unable to handle the children's lunches. I had to sit outside to get some air. I was sweating, nauseous and grumpy.

Lisa and Judith came out to join me.

'What's up, Jacky? You don't look yourself at all today.'

'Oh, nothing really,' I replied. 'It's rotten being pregnant.'

* * *

Resting on the bed after school that day, I was willing my stomach to settle, when Omar appeared and began kissing my neck and stroking my hair. I pulled away instantly.

'No, Omar, please.'

He stopped, surprised, then smiled and pulled me towards him once more. I sat up and pushed him firmly off me.

'Omar, I said no. I'm not feeling very well.'

It happened in a split second. Omar was no longer the man I knew. His eyes pierced through me as he frowned darkly so that his features changed completely.

He stood up and pointed at me. 'So, the teacher gives her children orders, and now she comes home to give her husband orders too.'

He bent down and took my face roughly in one hand, his face close to mine. 'Well, I am not about to listen to your orders, not now or ever. Are you listening to me? Do you understand?'

His tone was suddenly terrifying. He was like a stranger.

'Yes. I understand,' I whispered back, averting my eyes from his and trying to twist my face away.

'Look at me when I'm speaking to you,' he bellowed, so loudly that I immediately relaxed my face and looked back at him obediently.

'Yes, Omar.'

'A good wife never refuses her husband. Never. Do you understand?' This time, his voice dropped to a loud whisper, so that he was hissing out the words. Spittle was oozing out of one corner of his mouth, and his breath stank of cigarettes. I really thought I was going to throw up all over him.

'Now lie down,' he said, pushing me back down on the bed, 'and lift up your skirt.'

I was too bewildered to protest. I lay there as he pressed his sweaty body against mine, and roughly had sex, grunting and gyrating, thrusting harder and deeper until I couldn't bear him close to me. The nausea was caught in my throat and I could hardly breathe. At that moment, he was disgusting to me. He was filthy and he made me feel filthy.

And then it was over. He got up to leave. 'That is a lesson from me to you. If you want to be a good wife, then learn from it.'

I rolled over onto my side and curled up into a little ball. Questions were flying around my head. How had all that started? How had I let him do that to me? Why did he do it to me? But most of all, I asked myself, 'Who was the man who was in the bedroom just now with me?'

The bile rose in my throat as I sat, trying to make sense of everything. I rushed to the bathroom and was sick. It was a blessed release. I sat coughing and spitting into the toilet bowl, waiting for the feeling of nausea to subside and taking deep breaths. When I felt a strong hand on my shoulder, I froze. It was Omar.

'Come, darling, you need a shower. You will feel much better.'

I looked up. Gone were the glazed, mad eyes of a stranger. In their place were the deep, brown, smiling eyes that belonged to my husband. Puzzled, but too weak to work it out, I allowed myself to be undressed, showered and put into a *galabeya*.

'If you are feeling tired, then I will ask Mama to let us eat with the family, so that you do not have to cook.'

'I'm not hungry myself. You go and eat. I will join you later.'

I lifted my face so that he could kiss my cheek, and he went through to the kitchen to check on the progress of his meal. I could hear him humming as he clashed the saucepan lids down.

As I crept back along the dark corridor, Salma appeared and whisked me into her room.

'Jacky, are you all right?'

I looked at her, unsure as to what she meant. Had she heard me being sick, or Omar shouting?

She continued, not waiting for a reply. 'Mervette was very sick when she was having her baby. Mama will make you something to help it go away.'

'Thank you,' I replied. Her kindness suddenly made me want to cry, and before I could stop it, a tear rolled down my cheek, and spilled onto her arm.

'My brother has a very angry temper,' she said.

Despite myself, I smiled. 'You mean a very bad temper, Salma.'

'Yes. He shouts and breaks things many times. He is the naughty one in our family. He fights with Papa for what he wants, even though we should never, ever shout at Papa.'

I looked up at her. 'Like when he wanted to marry me?'

'Yes,' she answered, 'like that. You must try to be a good wife, Jacky. He loves you very much. He would die for you, I am sure. But do not make him angry with you. Do you understand?'

'Yes, Salma, I understand.'

I hugged this young girl, wise beyond her years, and was thankful that she was there for me. Her concern for me as her sister was genuine, and she was trying so hard to be tactful.

I decided that I must try harder. I should not have pushed Omar away, no matter how sick I felt. His needs must now be my prime consideration, and then he would always love me.

19

On the Move

The weekend for us was Friday and Saturday, Friday being the day of worship for Moslems. The working week began on Sunday.

That weekend, I continued to suffer from morning sickness that lasted all day long. Mama gave me a milky drink that was supposed to be the best cure, but it had little effect.

At first Mama was sympathetic, but as Saturday evening drew on and I had done nothing to help around the house, her patience began to wear out. My knowledge of Arabic was improving daily, and I was becoming used to the way she spoke. I was now able to understand when she complained to Omar that I was lazy and should start to pull my weight. She failed to mention that I hadn't eaten a thing since Wednesday.

I went to work on Sunday morning feeling marginally better, having managed a cup of tea. It was wonderful to be driven away from the claustrophobic, unwelcoming flat to the company of bright, happy children and understanding friends.

Karen returned to school that day. She had been off for the last week, and was very reserved during the morning. The heat was beginning to be oppressive now that we were in May, and we all wore short-sleeved dresses or blouses at work. The Egyptian staff usually draped a thin veil over their head and shoulders, and I had a cardigan and a scarf to wear when I went to and from school. Karen, however, had a woollen, polo-necked jumper over a long skirt.

At lunchtime I had the chance to ask her how she was.

'I don't know, Jacky, I really don't think I can carry on like this much longer.'

'Why? What's happened?'

Glancing furtively around to make sure we were alone, she pulled down the neck of her jumper to reveal large areas of bruising, dark purple with tinges of green beginning to appear.

I gasped. 'Did Samir . . . ?' I trailed off.

She nodded. 'At first it was the odd push or slap. But now the slightest thing sends him crazy. I've had to wear these clothes because he cut up everything of mine in the flat he could find. Now I have nothing.'

'Oh, Karen, how awful.' I put my arm around her. 'I have a few dresses and we're both about the same size. I'll bring a couple in tomorrow for you.'

'Thanks. I'm really grateful. He's hidden my passport as well. He thinks I'll leave him.'

'Why do you stay? You can't be happy like this.'

'I love him.' She paused. 'And he loves me. He's studying for his finals at the moment and he gets stressed so easily.'

'So is Omar,' I replied. 'We used to go out for romantic walks and talk most evenings, but now he's immersed in his books. We don't talk much any more.'

Karen flinched as she stood up to see the clock through the classroom window.

'What's the matter with your back?' I asked.

'He flung me against the cooker and I hurt it. I have a nasty bruise all down here.' She pointed to her lower back on one side.

'Karen, you have to do something. He can't be allowed to do this.'

'After his exams, there'll be no reason for him to get angry,' she replied dully. 'Come on, we have to be back in a couple of minutes.'

Over the next couple of weeks, Karen and I became closer, while Mama and I grew further apart. Every day, on my return from school, she would ask me to do a particular chore, in return for her allowing Omar and me to eat with the family.

I was still nauseous and eating very little. I was even unable to make tea without my stomach turning. Cooking smells and cigarette smoke affected me the most. So I was given the washing to do – for the whole family.

The local washing powder came in tiny boxes the size of a Paxo stuffing box. It was called Rabso and it was allowed to be used only for clothes, and very sparingly. In order to wash sheets and towels, I had to fill the bath with cold water, take a grater and grate a bar of rough brown soap into it, swirling it round with a wooden stick. Then I'd add the washing, push it up and down, leave it for an hour or so and go back to rinse it.

The rinsing was the worst part. The towels were heavy and I couldn't squeeze them out properly. It took ages as I knelt over the bath, emptying and refilling the bath and finally squeezing the sheets. My back and knees killed me, yet there was still more to be done. I had to pile the wet washing into a large plastic tub and haul it through to the back bedroom. Pushing back the shutters, I would open the windows to hang everything out on the lines strung outside the window.

It had to be the back bedroom, as the flat was built on a corner, and that was the only window that faced the side street. The others faced directly out onto the main road, and would get dirty from all the dust and fumes from the traffic.

Mama seemed to want to make my life a misery. If I hung out the washing first, she would come up behind me shouting that the bathroom needed cleaning. If I left the washing in the bedroom and went to clear up the bathroom first, she would complain that I had just left the washing for someone else to hang out.

Every time I declined to eat, she took this as a personal insult, telling me to cook for myself if I didn't like it.

It was no use telling Omar any of this. He was oblivious to us all as the dates of his final exams drew nearer. Karen and I quietly told each other everything.

One lunchtime we were sitting in the garden at school while the children were playing. For a change I had some news.

'Mervette and Tarek move into their flat tomorrow, and her mother has bought her lots of beautiful furniture. They've even got a water heater.'

'How about your flat, Jacky? Are you any closer to moving out?'

'No,' I replied. 'The workmen have been working on Tarek's to get it finished. It'll be ages yet and, in the meantime, I'm cracking up living under the same roof as my mother-in-law.'

Karen sat thinking and then turned to me and grabbed my shoulders excitedly. 'That's it! Jacky, I've just had the most brilliant idea. You can't stand living where you are. I'm scared living alone with Samir when he's so stressed. He wants to study and so does Omar. So why don't you both move in with us for a while?'

I shrugged. 'They'd never agree.'

'Why not? It makes perfect sense. Look, I'll suggest it to Samir tonight, if you promise to do the same to Omar.'

'I promise.'

The next day, I was bursting to get to school and see Karen.

'Karen, you'll never believe this, but he agreed straightaway. Mama's been driving him mad as well, complaining about me, nagging him to do things, interrupting him all the time. What did Samir say?'

'He said they knew each other from university and got on well. He thought it was a good idea. They can study in peace, while we spend time together without bothering them. Oh Jacky, can you believe this is happening?'

She flung her arms around me and we hugged for a long time.

*　　*　　*

Mama was furious. She ranted at Omar, hitting him over the head and speaking so fast I couldn't grasp any of it. She became so violent that Mohamed and Salma had to restrain her. Magda joined in, hands on hips next to Mama. Eventually Papa roared at everyone and sent them all off into different rooms.

Omar packed a couple of bags, snatched the car keys off the side table and we left – there and then – to go and stay with Samir and Karen.

'Why was Mama so angry?' I asked.

'Tarek has just left and now I want to go. She will miss us.'

'I would have thought she'd be glad to see the back of me.'

'It's just her way.'

He never referred to the incident again.

20

Behind Closed Doors

Samir made us very welcome. He was polite to me and got
on very well with Omar, although they had different
natures and were completely different to look at. Samir was
very tall and well-built with thick, black hair and a moustache.
He had piercing black eyes and his skin was dark. Omar's skin
was fair in comparison; he even had a few freckles. Although
their hair was the same length and style, Omar's was brown,
almost auburn to match his eyes. Samir had a formidable look
about him that I found very intimidating, whereas Omar was
friendly and more approachable. It was hard to believe they
were both twenty-four. Samir could have been ten years older.

They soon got into a routine of studying together, which left
Karen and me to our own devices. Karen and Samir had the
flat completely to themselves; Samir's parents were dead and
his two sisters had married and moved out. It was on the
ground floor, with three large bedrooms and two reception
rooms. It was sparsely furnished, with the exception of a huge
ornate dresser in one of the living-rooms and a lavish dressing-
table with an enormous mirror in a carved wooden frame in
the main bedroom. The kitchen was overrun with cockroaches.

The pipe had cracked and sewage from the whole block was constantly trickling down the outside of the pipe and ending up outside Karen's kitchen. The stench was overpowering and put us off preparing food.

'This is disgusting. You need a handkerchief over your face to even set foot in here,' I said when Karen showed me round. 'When are they going to fix it?'

Karen sighed. 'Who knows? Two men did turn up last week, but then left again. All they ever say to Samir is *bokra*.'

I laughed. 'You certainly learn how to be patient in this country. Everything is always *bokra*, and tomorrow never comes.'

Over the next week, Omar went back and forth from Papa's flat to Samir's, until we had all our possessions with us. The flats were only a few streets away from each other, in the same area of Cairo, and it would have been easy for any of the family to visit us, but no one came.

During the first week of living together, it was clear that Karen lived in fear of Samir. She was a quiet, gentle-natured girl, always softly spoken, yet he shouted at her constantly and ordered her about. When they were together she scuttled around him, fetching him this or that, her face pinched and nervous. I asked Omar why he thought Samir was like this towards Karen, but he only shrugged and told me not to interfere.

When she spent time alone with me she relaxed and was funny, intelligent and good company. It was a pleasure to paint each other's nails. I had never painted my toenails before marrying Omar and I found it difficult to do it neatly. There was no choice in this matter; it was expected that when we went out we looked smart and that included make-up and nail varnish. Appearances were of the utmost importance, even if they were false ones.

It was May now. My nausea had disappeared and I felt surprisingly well. My spirits lightened and I was optimistic for the future. Money was the only blight on the horizon and, just like Samir and Karen, it was a struggle for us to earn enough to live on.

Shortly after moving in, all four of us went for an evening walk along the banks of the Nile. The men walked ahead chatting and we followed closely behind. I linked my arm through Karen's and lifted up my head to breathe in the smells of the evening. The smell of sewage in the flat was worse than ever and it felt good to get outside.

'Oh, it smells so good. Let's buy some yams. I feel like something sweet,' I said.

'Oh yes. Samir, can we afford to buy yams?' Karen followed suit and lifted up her head to the night air. As she did so, Samir swung around and smacked her hard across her face.

'No yams. We must go back now.'

Karen had accepted the blow without a word. Her face revealed no emotion as she lowered her head, putting one hand up to where her face was stinging. 'I'm so sorry, Samir. I forgot.'

Samir grabbed her hand and turned to smile politely at Omar. 'You two go on. We'll see you later.'

They shook hands and Samir turned to me. 'Goodnight, Jacky.'

I nodded and looked at the ground. Omar put his arms around my shoulders and we continued, leaving Karen to her fate.

'Why did he hit her? Why is he so cruel? Did she embarrass him because he couldn't afford the yams?' I stopped, deep in thought. 'We should go back with them. What if he hits her again?'

'We cannot,' Omar explained. 'We must never interfere between husband and wife. He won't hit her again. He was only reminding her to be a good, respectable wife. It wasn't the yams.'

I still didn't understand. 'But she tries so hard to do everything right. What did she forget?'

'She looked up. She should always keep her eyes downward. Enough now,' he continued, 'do you still want a yam?'

'No, let's save the money.'

I had lost my appetite. We walked for a short while, but then turned round and went back to the flat. It was in darkness. We crept around preparing for bed and lay in each other's arms. Omar was soon asleep, but I stayed awake for a long time, listening to the quiet sobbing in the next room and waiting for it to stop.

The following morning, I went to fetch the glasses from the sitting-room to make tea, the wife's first job of the day. There was an opened bottle of Johnny Walker on the table, and one of the glasses still smelled of whisky. I took the glasses into the kitchen to wash them when Karen appeared, dressed for school with sunglasses, and a scarf wrapped around her face. I opened my mouth to ask her how she was, but she put a finger to her red lips to silence me.

Once on the bus, she opened up. 'If Samir were to overhear us talking about him, things would only be worse for me. You have to make him believe we don't ever talk about him or he will make you leave.'

'I could hear you crying last night. Did he hit you again?' I asked.

'No. I kept saying how sorry I was. He shouted some more and sent me to bed. Then he started on the whisky. When he heard you come in, he switched off the lights and came to bed.'

'I thought Moslems weren't supposed to drink alcohol,' I said, but even as I spoke, I remembered that Papa kept several bottles of whisky in the cupboard; I'd seen them when I'd put his pyjamas away.

'Oh, Samir's very crafty,' Karen replied. 'He always drinks in private.'

'He's crafty all right,' I said. 'It's the same with the way he treats you. He's got you right where he wants you.'

'He's not like that all the time. He can be lovely. I know he loves me.'

'If he loves you, he doesn't show it,' I said. 'You don't seem happy to me. Look me in the eyes and tell me you are.'

The bus turned into the school entrance. Karen looked away.

*　　*　　*

It was pay-day. We returned to the flat with our money. Samir was at the door to greet us, a smile on his face. 'I have a surprise for you.'

He had bought a large cake. He cut four generous slices and handed them round. We sat down to eat.

Karen got up. 'I'll fetch some forks.'

Samir's face darkened. 'Sit down,' he barked.

The colour drained from Karen's face as she slowly sat down again.

'I bought the cake. I will get the forks.' Samir strode out of the room, returning with four forks. He gave out two and sat next to Karen. She tried to take her fork, but he grabbed her by the wrist. 'You want to make me look small in front of our friends? You think I want them to eat their cake with their fingers? Like this?'

He grabbed her cake and began to force it into her mouth. When she struggled, he wrenched her head back by her long hair and smeared cake over her cheeks.

'Happy birthday, wife,' he said, and turned to Omar. 'Let's go and study. She needs to clean herself up.'

He shoved her roughly away from him, stood up and brushed himself down. Omar put his plate down and they left the room. I ran to hug her as she sobbed quietly into my shoulder.

'What did he say? Happy birthday? Is it your birthday today, Karen?'

She nodded miserably. 'I'm twenty-one today. I'd completely forgotten.'

'I wish he'd forgotten,' I muttered.

'Where has the love gone?' she whispered. 'You're right, Jacky. I can't stay here much longer. And now I don't have to.' She wiped cream from her face defiantly on the armchair.

'What do you mean?'

Karen was immediately more confident. 'I know where he's hidden my passport. It's in the lining of the jacket he married me in. All I need now is the fare.'

'How will you get it?' I was intrigued.

'From my mother. I'll telephone her from school. She can send the money there and I'll leave before Samir has a chance to realise what's going on.' She leaned forward and kissed me. 'Oh Jacky, I am really going to go through with this.'

That night, in bed with Omar, we listened once again to Samir shouting at Karen. I took Omar's hand and guided it over my swelling stomach to let him feel the little fluttery movements, which had recently started.

'Hello, son,' he whispered.

'You're so sure it will be a boy, aren't you?' I said.

'Of course it's a boy. My son. Adham.'

'And if it's a girl?' I asked. 'What will her name be?'

'Trust me, it's a boy,' he replied.

'We don't have any spare money, do we?' I asked.

'Don't worry,' he replied. 'I will buy you gold after my exams.'

'I wasn't thinking about gold.'

'Every husband should buy his wife gold, to show how wealthy they are,' he said.

'I was thinking about the cost of a doctor and a hospital, and all the drugs,' I said.

'All these things will be a lot of money. I will have to ask Papa.'

'But Papa is angry that we have left. He will never agree to give us money.' I sat up to face him. 'Omar, I've had an idea.'

He pulled me back under the blanket. 'You'll get cold, *habibti*. Tell me your idea.'

'What if I asked *my* father to send us the airfares so I can have our baby in England? Everything is free there. And my mother would be there,' I added quietly, 'which would be really nice for me. I miss her so much.'

Omar looked into my eyes, smiling. 'That is a very good idea. But I need a visa to travel.'

'Can I telephone to England? If I take money from my wages, Mrs Sellar will let me use the phone at school.'

'Yes, do this tomorrow, and I will see about a visa. Send my love to your parents.'

It was as easy as that. Karen and I were both excited as we began making plans. She telephoned her mother in West Lothian, Scotland, and arranged to leave at the end of June, in another month. She also informed Mrs Sellar of her intentions, handing in her resignation secretly.

I telephoned home and Dad agreed straightaway to send the fares. It was all brilliant timing, as Samir didn't suspect a thing. He assumed my excitement was rubbing off on Karen.

As the final exams drew closer, Samir became more nervous than ever, resulting in terrible tantrums and arguments with

Karen over the slightest thing. Finally, after another couple of tense weeks, Omar admitted to me that he could no longer stand the atmosphere. He couldn't study and decided to return to his father's flat.

I wasn't asked for my opinion. He just told me to put our things into bags to be fetched later and to say goodbye to Karen and Samir.

There was no time for goodbyes. Five minutes later we were standing outside on the street while Omar hailed a taxi. The Peugeot belonged to Papa and Omar had left no time to borrow it. The local taxis were little black-and-white cars and there was always one passing by so we didn't have to wait long.

Omar opened the back door for me and then jumped into the passenger seat to chat to the driver. After only a few minutes, the driver nodded at Omar and leered at me through his mirror, showing his filthy teeth and raising his eyebrows. He asked Omar if I was a Moslem. In an instant, Omar lashed out and grabbed the driver round the neck. There was a screech as he swerved and hit the brakes to stop the car. I was thrown onto my side and, as I sat up again, Omar was already out of the taxi, dragging the driver from his seat.

I watched in horror. They were on the pavement now. The driver had his hands clasped tightly in front of him and seemed to be pleading. He was big and fat, but frightened of the fury in Omar's eyes. Omar grasped the driver's shoulders and head-butted him on his forehead. This knocked the driver clean out and he fell heavily to the ground with a grunt. Omar pushed his body roughly over until he rolled into the gutter, his eyes staring eerily upwards, his face covered in dust. Blood trickled down his cheek and dripped onto his *galabeya*.

I looked around, expecting someone to offer to help the poor man. But the people just hurried past, women ushering their children to keep up. Some men had stopped to watch, yet none of them interfered or questioned Omar as he dusted himself down and straightened his shirt. He opened the taxi door for me to get out and stopped another taxi, leaving the driver in the gutter and the meter in his vehicle still ticking over.

By now I knew when it was time to keep quiet, and this was certainly one of those times. I tried to justify his behaviour to myself. He was protecting me, I told myself. He doesn't want a stranger asking questions about his pregnant wife and staring at her in his mirror. It's because he loves me.

But throughout that journey I felt very nervous at the way Omar had lost control. It reminded me too much of Samir. 'But he isn't like that with me. I must always remember that,' I thought.

21

Wife and Mother

When we returned to live with Omar's family, Mama was sullen and unfriendly. There was no longer a room for us. Our room had been turned into a study for Mohamed and his friend, who was staying with him. Omar would have to sleep with them, while I was told to bed down with Salma and Magda.

Magda was preoccupied with the idea of marriage; a man she liked had approached Papa for her hand and discussions were taking place. She would have to wait for the outcome to see if he would be her husband or not. Tarek and Mervette now lived in their flat in Embaba with their baby son, Ahmed. Only Salma made us feel welcome, giving me a hug and a smile. I resigned myself to the strained days that undoubtedly stretched before me, knowing that soon I would be flying out of there to my lovely home in England.

At school, Karen kept me up to date with her plans. I had been worried that she would give up and decide to try again when I moved out, but Samir's behaviour was getting more erratic and unpredictable. One day he had ripped the plug off the television and smashed the radio cassette player against the wall. On another he had lost his temper and left the house in a rage, completely trashing the place on his return.

'I wish I was still with you so that you didn't have to face it on your own,' I said in the staff room one day.

'It makes no difference any more,' she replied. 'Every time he loses his temper, I get stronger.'

'Just make sure to get out before he kills you.'

Omar failed to obtain a visa to travel with me. He had not yet completed his National Service. He was advised to marry me at the British Embassy to give him a better chance. We were able to do this on a Friday, as it was not a holiday for the embassy. The ceremony was quick, unimpressive and expensive. It did not work. Omar was once more refused a visa, so the whole process had been a total waste of time and money. It cost £30.50, almost a month's wages for me.

We sat together in the back of the Peugeot holding hands as Mohamed drove us back to the flat.

'What shall we do?' I asked miserably.

'You will have to travel without me,' replied Omar. 'I will finish my exams and start work on our flat. Then you can come back to your new home.'

We booked my ticket for the end of June. In two weeks. Omar's exams began, and he needed to study whenever he was at home. Although I understood this, Mama didn't. She was forever interrupting them in the 'study', or making too much noise with Magda in the next room.

I had more chores than ever, but in my spare time I would sit quietly writing letters home, filling them with stories of how exciting my life was in Egypt and how I couldn't wait to have a son and bring him back. The last thing I wanted was for my parents to worry. I was worried enough myself. The job was fine, but I would never survive living under the same roof as Mama. I needed a place of our own. But if we were on our own, how would I look after a new baby? I'd never had one before. It wasn't like a new kitten or a budgie. It didn't come with instructions. I was torn between wanting support and struggling on my own. Whatever the future held, I was secretly dreading it.

'Eh baadayn!'

I was shaken out of my reverie by the sound of Omar crashing out of the study to confront Mama, who was watching television in the front sitting-room with the volume turned right up. I crept along the corridor to see what was going on. He strode over to the TV and switched it off, shouting at Mama and throwing his arms in the air. She began to shout back. Mohamed joined in, siding with Omar.

Still shouting, the men went back to study, slamming the door behind them. In defiance, like a child, Mama switched the TV back on and turned up the volume again. There was a loud bang from the room. And then nothing. The TV blared out, Mama left the room and I turned it down to an acceptable level and went back to my writing.

Omar had caused the bang. He had punched the door. It had splintered from the inside, and his hand was badly swollen.

I knew better than to raise the subject. It was another incident that was never referred to again.

A week before my departure, Omar came into the house and presented me with a long box.

'Open it. It's a present.'

It was a gold chain with the letters L, O, V and E shaped into a gold figure. Omar placed it round my neck and did up the clasp.

'Gold for my wife. You must go to England with some gold. When I have more money you can choose some gold earrings. The gold is better in Egypt.'

He was right. It was high quality and the chain was eighteen-carat. Most of the women I had seen wore several chains around their necks and bangles on their wrists. I was delighted that he'd bothered.

'I love it. I'll always wear it.'

At school on the last day of term, everyone made a fuss of me. It was the custom for parents to buy the teachers gifts, but I had no idea how seriously they regarded it. I received beautiful, expensive presents of gold, photo frames, ornaments, skeins of silk, papyrus, perfume, baby clothes and much more. I was completely overwhelmed. I was given a lot of letters to post when I got to England, as the post in Egypt was so unreliable. There was a big cake in the staff room for the occasion.

'Guess what?' Karen leaned towards me, speaking quietly. 'I leave in ten days, *inshallah*, and the men mended the pipe yesterday.'

I smiled. 'Somehow I don't think it's a good enough reason to stay, do you? Be strong, Karen. Take care not to give anything away in these final few days. Here.'

I gave her my address and telephone number in England written on a piece of paper.

'Thanks, Jacky. I can't wait to get out of here.'

England was green, wet, cloudy and beautiful. I had never really noticed how many different shades of green there were in the trees, bushes and hedges. The gentle summer rain glistening on the leaves made the colours stand out even more, and the smell of damp wood and pine needles was intoxicating.

It was an emotional homecoming for all three of us. Mum and Dad drove to London to meet me and enveloped me with bearhugs. At home we talked long into the night. I told them all about my job and the new friends I had made. They were very proud that I was a teacher. I talked a lot about Omar, but I left out the details of daily life under Mama's roof.

After seven months in Cairo, I found it very hard to get used to the way of life in England. I had eased myself gradually into life in Egypt, and returning home highlighted the differences acutely. The most striking difference was the lack of noise. The tranquillity of living in a village without the constant hum of traffic was a huge change. The birds singing, the sound of rain falling and, in contrast, the lack of the *adhan* crackling out on cassette from the tops of minarets five times a day made me realise what I had begun to accept as normal.

A shower each morning was all I needed to stay fresh all

day, without sweat running down my face at regular intervals and my hair sticking to me. I could have a bath and read the paper. We had time for conversation and I could catch a bus into town and do a little shopping and have a coffee whenever I felt like it. The day was not dominated by washing rice or cleaning floors with filthy sacks. I could go out alone to meet friends. It was normal life but it felt wonderful.

I attended antenatal classes and began buying baby clothes. I made sure to get several dozen terry nappies, as I knew we would never be able to afford disposable nappies in Egypt. Pampers were available in the supermarkets, but way beyond our means.

The baby was due at the beginning of November. I had travelled to England at the end of June and had four months to the birth.

I wrote to Omar regularly and he did his best to reply in English. I also tried to phone weekly. But this was both frustrating and unsatisfactory. The telephone system in Egypt was unreliable and it took ages to get through. Sometimes I didn't manage it at all and sometimes when I did, Omar wasn't there. When he was there, the line went dead before Mama handed him the phone. On the occasions I did manage to get through, I asked him about the flat and each time he had the same reply, 'Soon, very soon.' It was Salma who told me that Omar had passed his exams and from mid-July I was unable to speak to him at all. I cursed the telephone system and looked forward instead to his letters.

I was glad to be back in the comfort of my parents' home

and grateful that I didn't have to endure the interminable heat of the summer in Cairo while I was pregnant. I was also happy that my mum would be with me at the birth and that both Mum and Dad would see their first grandchild. Maternity care was the best in the world and the nurses and doctors spoke English, which was reassuring. In fact my life would have been perfect but for the fact that I missed Omar terribly.

In August it was my birthday. I was twenty-four. I tried to telephone several times, but when I eventually got through, Omar was not at home. I cried over the phone because I missed him so much, and promised Salma to take pictures of our son as soon as he was born. I had to make special arrangements with the doctor for the baby to be circumcised, to comply with the Islamic custom.

Throughout the last months of pregnancy, although my stomach ballooned, I felt healthy and well. A week before the due date, the pains began and on the last day in October, I gave birth to the most beautiful little girl that anyone had ever seen. I was shocked. The family had so convinced me that I was carrying a boy that it had never occurred to me that there was another possibility. I wondered briefly if they would be angry or disappointed, but to me she was like a miracle. I gazed at her for a long while, until the nurse allowed my parents and grandparents in to say hello. She was white, with long legs, a mop of brown hair and the most beautiful deep-blue eyes.

Later that day, I telephoned Egypt. Again, Omar was not there. I told Salma that I'd had the baby early and to tell her brother that he was now a papa. The family were ecstatic, shouting *mabrouk* down the line all at once.

'Tell me,' said Salma, 'what does he look like?'

'Well for a start, he isn't a *he*, he's a *she*,' I replied. 'Tell Omar we have a daughter. She is absolutely beautiful and she looks just like her papa.'

There was a lot of chatter at the other end of the phone while Salma relayed this information to the rest of the family. Then she said, '*Mabrouk*, Jacky. Are you all right?'

'A bit delicate. I haven't done this before, remember,' I answered. 'There is a problem though. Omar and I had only agreed on a name for a boy. We can't call her Adham now, can we? Have you any ideas?'

I waited until Salma eventually replied, 'Papa says that you can choose a name, as long as it will fit in here. I cannot wait to see you both. We all miss you, Jacky.'

'I can fly when she is six weeks old, so it won't be long now. Send my love to everyone. Tell Omar I love him.'

I chose the name Leila and before registering it officially, I rang Omar to be sure that it was suitable. Once again he was out. Tentatively I told Salma my chosen name. She just had time to say that she approved when we were cut off.

I stayed in the maternity home for a week, before returning home. Mum had put notice of the birth in the local paper, and I was inundated with visits, everyone bringing flowers for me and presents for Leila. Cards full of good wishes arrived from friends who lived away and my grandparents fussed and cooed delightedly over this new addition to the family.

One cold, bright morning, sitting in the bay window in the front room with Leila wrapped up against the cold November air, I had closed my eyes and was about to doze off when I felt a hand on my shoulder. It was Mum.

'Jacky, there's someone to see you.'

I sat up, rubbing my eyes. It was Karen. I couldn't believe it. She was smiling from ear to ear, her red hair in a ponytail and she was dressed in smart winter clothes. She held out her arms and I stood up to give her a big hug.

'It's so good to see you. Oh Karen, you made it. How did you know I was here? Why didn't you phone before making such a long journey?'

'I did. Only I asked your mum to keep it a secret. I wanted to surprise you. I can stay for the weekend, if that's all right?'

'All right? Of course it's all right. I'll put the kettle on and then you must come and see Leila while she's sleeping.'

'Didn't Omar have his heart set on having a son?' Karen asked.

'He doesn't mind,' I replied, 'and at least she doesn't have to be circumcised.'

Karen was suddenly serious. 'That's not strictly true. Samir's elder sister was, but the younger one got away with it somehow. It's an old custom. In the villages it is always done and there are still families in Cairo who strongly believe in it too.'

'But that's awful . . .'

'Just be careful, Jacky.'

I shuddered. 'There's no chance anyone will do such a thing to my daughter. They'd have to kill me first.'

Karen had arrived in England a week after me. Samir had been so wrapped up in himself that he hadn't given a thought to how Karen was feeling. It had been easy for her to slip away.

'He knows where I am now, but what can he do? It's too late for him to say he'll change.'

'But what if he decides to come to Scotland? You lived there together before.'

'Yes, I know, but when we moved to Cairo he changed. I never want to see him again.'

I looked down at Leila. 'At least you don't have any children. That would have complicated things.'

'It's over.' Karen looked at me unwaveringly. She possessed an inner strength that put conviction into her soft voice.

I handed Leila to her for a cuddle. 'I'm glad.'

In fact Karen did question my intention to return. She wasn't alone. Mum and Dad were under great emotional strain. They had been through this once before. It was that time of year again with Christmas approaching. We did some shopping, buying a Moses basket, feeding bottles, a steriliser and boxes of sterilising tablets. I chose some material and Mum made the cover for the basket with a hood. She also bought me a baby-bouncing chair, which came apart and would easily fit into a suitcase.

Leila was three weeks old before I realised that I had forgotten to register her birth. With the confusion over choosing a name it had slipped my mind. Dad took me to the registry office, and it was there that I decided to name her after my mum as well. So my baby officially became Leila Anne. If we had had a son, he would have taken both Omar and Papa's names. That was the custom, Omar had told me. But since we had a daughter, I saw no reason to burden her with two male names, so I discarded them without a second thought. This was another big mistake, for which, unknowingly, I would pay heavily.

One week before returning to Cairo, I received a letter from Omar saying that the flat in Embaba was ready. I saw this as a good omen, a chance for a whole new life for the three of us. I flew back full of optimism and enthusiasm.

But when I arrived at Cairo airport with my new baby, Omar was not there.

22

Hard Times

Mohamed was at the airport to meet us. He lifted Leila up gently and smothered her in kisses, before handing her back and attending to our luggage.

'*Fayn Omar?*' I asked, my eyes desperately searching the car park as we approached the car.

Mohamed spoke neither English nor French. '*Omar geh bade shwiya, bi layl.*'

I was astounded. Where was he? Why couldn't he come to meet us? As far as I could make out, Mohamed had said he was coming in the evening. What was more important than meeting his wife and seeing his daughter for the first time?

We sat in silence on the journey back to Papa's flat. When we arrived, the family was there but not Omar. One after the other they picked up Leila and threw her into the air again and again. She had been sleeping peacefully. Naturally this was a terrible shock to her and she began to cry. So they handed her back to me, saying she was hungry.

'Salma, where is Omar?' I managed to ask amid the din.

'He's in the army. He's coming tonight.'

I escaped with Leila to a bedroom to breastfeed and think.

I was beginning to panic now, but I couldn't do anything until Leila had settled.

Half an hour passed and Salma came in. 'Are you hungry? The food is ready. Come and eat.'

She bent down, took Leila from me and put her deftly over her shoulder to wind her.

'Salma, tell me about Omar. What did you mean by army? Is there a war?'

'No. He has finished university. He must go in the army. Everyone has to.'

Finally I understood. Omar had been called up for National Service. 'But where is he? How long will he be away? When did he go?'

'July, after you left for England. He must stay for fifteen months. He is in Fayoum near Suez and Ismailia.'

I stared at her, working things out in my mind. 'So all those times I tried to call and he was never there . . .' I trailed off.

'He was away,' said Salma. 'He didn't want you to worry.'

'Worry? Why would I be worried? Is he in danger?' I was confused now.

'No, no. He is coming to see you now. He will be here soon.'

Leila gave a loud burp and went to sleep on Salma's shoulder. I tucked her into the Moses basket. 'Let's go and eat. Will he be here for long?'

'I'm not sure,' replied Salma vaguely.

* * *

After eating, I opened one of the two suitcases I had brought back and took all the presents for the family into Papa's room. We all sat together on his bed and I gave them out. Polo shirts for Mohamed, long-sleeved fancy blouses and underwear for Magda, a few novels in English and a trouser suit for Salma, three shorts and T-shirt sets for baby Ahmed, an electric manicure kit for Mervette, a jumper for Tarek. For Mama I had found a beautiful embroidered long cardigan with gilt buttons and a thick, tartan dressing-gown for Papa, complete with a bottle of Johnny Walker. My mum had helped me choose the presents and paid for them all. We had bought polo shirts and jeans for Omar.

They were all very grateful, shouting all at once, showing each other what they had and kissing me. Tarek, Mervette and Ahmed arrived in the middle of the excitement and they joined in this mad, happy time. Papa put on his dressing-gown and walked up and down the corridor. He hugged me and called me his daughter, 'Shokran benti'.

I was delighted that it was such a success. 'It's like Christmas, only they don't have Christmas, so it isn't.' I laughed at the thought as the *adhan* began outside and the men left to pray.

Later that evening, around seven o'clock, Omar arrived. He flung himself into my arms and we hugged for a long time. Mama was delighted to see him and scurried into the kitchen to heat up some food, while I led him into the bedroom to introduce him to his daughter.

He was overcome with emotion as he lifted her into his arms. She stirred and puckered up her tiny lips to suckle. He laughed, kissed her and handed her to me, a tear escaping from his eye and dripping onto her cheek.

'She's beautiful,' he whispered. '*Benti Leila Omar. Ahebbik toolombri min taht albi.*'

I wondered why he had called her Leila Omar. I could understand his Arabic quite easily now. He had told her that he would love her forever from the bottom of his heart.

He looked ridiculous in his so-called uniform. The jacket was far too small and stretched painfully across his chest, while the trousers hung on him. The boots were huge. They had been issued to him without checking the size, as it was all they had at the time.

After showering and praying, Omar and I left Leila in the flat and went out to be alone. We sat inside a riverside restaurant because it was unusually chilly, and drank Coke. He could stay for only two days, and would come home whenever he could after that. He had to remain in the army until September. It was now December. Money would be a problem. Omar earned only 6LE per month, about £2, which didn't even cover the cost of his cigarettes, let alone travelling back to see us each week.

I began to sob silently. I couldn't help it. I knew he would be angry with me for crying in public, but my dreams had been shattered and I didn't want to hear what he was telling me.

Omar wasn't cross. He put his arm gently around me. 'Don't cry, *habibti*. Mama will look after you.'

Abruptly I stopped snivelling and looked up at him. 'What do you mean? Isn't the flat ready for us? You told me the flat was ready.' I could feel the panic rising in my throat. I felt sick as he replied.

'You cannot stay there alone. You will stay with Mama until I finish the army, and then we can live together in the flat.'

I stood up, shaking my head, unable to believe what I was hearing. 'You promised me,' I whispered.

Omar hurriedly left some coins on the table for the drinks and followed me into the street. 'What? You want to live there alone?' he asked.

'No, I want to live there with my daughter. I want to be her mother. I wanted to be a family on our own, not just another of Mama's daughters.' I breathed in sharply, my shoulders sagged and I began to sob. 'Oh, Omar, why didn't you tell me you had to go into the stupid army? How will I manage without you? I only came back for you. I wish I were still in England.'

The silence that followed was enough to make me realise that I had gone too far. I had hurt him. We walked back without a word. Omar strode into Papa's bedroom and closed the door behind him. I fed and changed Leila. Mama had given me a saucepan to put the dirty terry nappies in to soak. I would sort them out in the morning, I decided. I was upset and frightened for the future. I said goodnight and tried to sleep in Salma's room.

Omar didn't wake me. Leila woke in the middle of the night and I crept into the sitting-room to feed her without disturbing anyone. She then slept through until morning. I was changing her nappy when Omar came in.

'Jacky, we go to the flat today. Papa has agreed. When I am away, Tarek and Mervette will look after you.' He bent down to tickle Leila and then picked her up. 'Get dressed. I will look after Leila Omar.'

Mohamed drove us all to Embaba. The children must have recognised Omar. They didn't rush up to the car but stole into the shadows and looked on from a distance. I carried Leila while the men brought the luggage. The steps of the building were dusty. There was no handrail. On the fourth floor, Mervette was standing at the entrance to her flat, smiling broadly. She ushered us inside and fussed over Leila. Her son Ahmed crawled onto the settee to see the baby. He was nearly a year old and had never seen a baby before.

Mervette picked Leila up. '*Rooh enti shoof she'ik. Ana ha o'od ma Leila.*'

I stood up. '*Shokran. Ha gehik bade shwiya.*' She was a considerate girl. I was grateful to have some time to see our new home. I stepped across the landing through our front door.

My excitement drained away as I looked around. The builders had put in windows and shutters. Apart from that, nothing was any different from my last visit. The place was covered in dust. As I walked around I left footprints on the stone floor. In the second bedroom there were still piles of bricks and timber against one wall. There wasn't a stick of furniture to be seen.

The men threw open the shutters, letting the sunlight stream through and bringing the heat with it. They put the luggage in the main bedroom. Omar turned to me. 'I will bring some things from Mama's. You wait with Mervette.' He kissed me briefly and was gone.

I sat on the floor to think. What did we need to be able to live here? I was determined not to let the situation beat me. I was never going back to live with Mama. After a few minutes, I went across to see Mervette and borrowed a plastic bowl, pieces of old sacking and a squidgie. I rolled up my sleeves and prepared to clean the floors. With the windows open, it was already hot. I turned on the tap over the sink to splash water on my face before starting work. Nothing happened. I tried the other tap and then the taps in the kitchen. Nothing. I wiped the sweat from my forehead with the back of my hand and returned to ask Mervette what to do.

She laughed when she saw me and led me into her bedroom where there was a huge mirror. I was filthy, my face streaked with dirt and a huge area of grime on my skirt from where I had been sitting on the floor. Then she took me into her bathroom. There were three large plastic bowls containing water. She filled my little bowl from one of these and at last I was able to make a start.

Omar and Mohamed returned with Salma. By then, I had washed the main sitting-room and bedroom floors and needed clean water to do any more.

They had brought a thin, single, straw-filled mattress, two blankets, a Primus stove and a single saucepan. It was the one

Mama had given me for the nappies. Two dirty nappies were still inside it.

'We must sleep on this until we get a bed. Tell Salma if you need anything and she can get it.'

I wasted no time and spoke to Salma in English. 'We have no water, and nothing to clean the flat with. It's so hot already and the flies are all over the walls. Could Mama spare a fan, do you think? Also we have no spoons or bowls. And Omar will need a prayer mat,' I added, thinking that if I asked for something related to Islam, I might gain more sympathy.

Salma turned and spoke rapidly in Arabic to Omar. Then she said, 'There is no water in the taps because the building has no pump to pump the water up. You must bring it from the tap in the street.'

I stared at her, unable to believe what she was saying. 'You mean we will never have water in the taps?'

She shrugged. 'Maybe in a few months they will put in a pump. I will go home with Mohamed and bring you these things. Omar will fetch water. I am happy for you, Jacky. You have a new home for your family.'

'Thank you,' I replied. I suddenly thought of something and called her back. 'Salma, how did Mervette manage to buy such beautiful furniture? She has everything she needs.'

'In our country, when two people marry, the man provides the flat and the woman provides the furniture.' She stepped up to me and wiped away a dirty smudge from my face with her handkerchief. 'Don't worry, Jacky. You will manage. I will be back soon.'

Omar disappeared again and returned with two huge plastic bowls. He took one down into the street and filled it from the public water tap. It took three men to carry it back up. Then he brought a sack of rice and a chicken. He was carrying it upside down by its legs and I assumed it was dead. I had the shock of my life when he let it go and it flapped wildly around, squawking.

'I will bring tomatoes and vegetables now,' he said, 'and we can eat.'

While he was away, I fed Leila in the comfort of Mervette's flat and put her to sleep in the bedroom. Mervette decided to help and together we were able to wash all the floors and get rid of the dust clinging to the walls and windowsills. I had no idea why Omar had brought a chicken, but was too preoccupied to worry about it. I named her Polly and shut her in the bathroom. In the kitchen, I had to put the sterilising set and Leila's bottles on the floor, as there were no cupboards or worktops. The rice went in one corner. I left all our clothes in the suitcases on the bedroom floor, and put the spongebag on the windowsill in the bathroom. To tempt the flies away, I pulled the shutters ajar leaving the windows open. I rolled the mattress out and put Leila's bouncing chair beside it.

We went back to Mervette's flat for tea. Salma, Mohamed and Omar returned and joined us. Salma had done quite well, although she hadn't managed to bring a fan. There was a box with utensils and four plastic bowls, four plates and an old tin lid that I could use to sort the rice. There were also two prayer mats, two sacks, an old kettle and a bag of tea.

Omar went across to our flat and wrung the chicken's neck. I was horrified when he returned holding up poor, dead Polly and asked me to come and prepare her. I got up and followed him into our kitchen, where he placed Polly, still warm, on the floor. 'You can do it here,' he said.

'Oh no,' I replied. 'You never said you were going to kill her. I might be hungry, but I'm not that hungry, and I'm certainly not going to eat Polly.'

'Polly? What is Polly?' Omar was confused. 'Papa brought the chicken for us. Why would I bring a chicken into our home? Of course it's to eat.'

'Polly is the name I gave her, because I thought she was here to keep for the eggs. No, Omar. I'm sorry, but I can't do it.' I was adamant.

So it was Omar who plucked, cleaned and boiled poor Polly. When I flatly refused to eat her, his patience snapped and he had his first temper tantrum. He ranted and raved in Arabic, smashing his fist into the wall. His eyes were flashing danger- ously. Leila began to cry. I picked her up and instinctively backed away. He put his hand under my chin and raised my face very close to his, saying things I couldn't understand. I could smell cigarettes on his breath. His hand smelt of Polly. I closed my eyes.

Suddenly he pushed me away and walked out, slamming the door behind him. I rocked Leila back and forth, crying silently and chastising myself. Why had I chosen a chicken over my husband? We were hot, dirty, hungry, desperately tired and broke. A chicken was a lovely gift and I had all but thrown it back in Papa's face. It was a huge insult. I had showed such lack of respect, which was unforgivable in Omar's eyes. Especially as he didn't know when the next piece of meat would pass our lips.

Half an hour passed and Omar returned.

'I'm sorry, I was stupid. It was all my fault,' I began, but he silenced me with a long kiss. As quickly as his temper had flared up it had disappeared. His eyes were soft and brown once more.

'Sssh,' he whispered. 'Don't worry. Put the chicken on a plate and Mervette will put it into the fridge.' He stroked my face and looked down at my grubby *galabeya*. 'We need a shower and some clean clothes. I'll ask Mohamed to take us with him when he goes home. We can take a taxi back.'

Later, we returned to Papa's where we ate and had a shower. It felt so luxurious to have cold water splashing over me and I was grateful to be able to wash my hair. But it didn't wash away the apprehension and fear growing inside me. I knew we couldn't go on like this. I also knew that Mama was waiting for us to crawl back with our tails between our legs and she would once again be in charge.

I made a decision. Boldly, in front of the rest of the family, I asked Mama if Leila and I could visit every Friday to eat with them and take a shower. Papa thought it was a good idea and Mama reluctantly agreed. We returned to Embaba by taxi without incident. I stared doggedly at the floor for the whole journey.

As the evening advanced and the sun went down, it became cold. The cool stone floors, which had been so welcome in the heat of the day, were now icy to the touch. It was far too cold to sleep in a *galabeya*, so we both left our clothes on. The mattress was too narrow for both of us and we had to take it in turns. When Omar returned to the army, I could have it for the whole night, but for now, I was resigned to huddling on the floor wrapped in a blanket, awaiting my turn and remembering my comfy bed lying empty at home in England. Making love was out of the question.

It was quiet in the flat at night, in total contrast to the noisy street where Papa lived. In the dark, I sat inside my blanket, watching my husband and daughter sleep. I was cold, uncomfortable in my clothes and terrified of what the future held. I wanted Omar to take me in his arms and tell me that everything would be fine. But in my heart I honestly didn't know how on earth it could ever be.

23

Home Sweet Home

The next day, I needed to wash Leila's nappies. There was only one saucepan and no washing powder. Omar went down to the *souk* and bought a bar of dull brown soap, a grater and a bag of white rocky chunks, which he called *butaas*. It was a form of acid. He lit the Primus stove and I boiled water in the pan, grated soap and added a chunk of *butaas*. I stirred the nappies with a stick left behind by the builders. After rinsing the nappies, they were as white as snow. Omar hammered two pieces of wood on the outside edges of the balcony and wrapped thick cord several times between them, creating ten washing lines. He borrowed pegs from Mervette and I was able to hang the nappies out to dry.

'You must take care to cover your hair when you go out onto the balcony,' Omar warned. 'You must not let others look at you.'

By the time I had attended to Leila and washed other bits of baby clothes and some underwear, it was midday. The heat was unforgiving, and we had to drink from a single glass, as Salma had not brought any from Papa's and Mervette could only spare one. I wondered if the water was safe to drink, but as there was no alternative, I saw little point in asking.

Omar had gone to see his Uncle Hassan, and returned with the news that Hassan had an old wardrobe and dressing-table we could have. Papa's men were still in the process of making cupboards for the kitchen. He would then start work on making a double bed for us and a cot for Leila.

I had arranged to return to work at the school, taking Leila with me. George had even agreed to make a special journey to collect us each day.

I was starting tomorrow, but right now I had the daunting task of providing my husband with a meal before he left to return to the army. I couldn't bring myself to cook food in the same saucepan I had used to boil the nappies, so I chopped some tomatoes, washed some cucumbers and sliced them in half. The tomatoes were huge and tasteless, yet the cucumbers were tiny and tasty.

Omar laughed when he saw the result of my efforts and went down to buy *fool* and bread and salt. This was the staple diet of all Egyptians and cost thirty piastres for the lot. *Fool* consisted of brown beans in a brown sauce. Traders cooked it daily in a huge pot and baked the bread on huge slabs. It was bland with a sloppy, revolting texture, but I was so hungry I swallowed a large mouthful. The *fool* and tomatoes tasted much better with salt. I ate a whole plateful with lots of bread and plenty of salad.

Omar was pleased to see me tucking in for a change. 'I have arranged for a boy to bring *fool*, *tarmeyer* and bread to our door every morning for your breakfast,' he said. 'I will pay him fifty piastres every week to do this. He will leave it outside the door, knock and leave. You must wait until he has gone before you open the door.'

'I'll need some money for some basics. Shall I ask for a loan at school?' I asked.

'No, it's better that I take it from Papa and then pay him from your school money later. Anyway, we have the *saboor* to think about.'

I looked up. 'What's a *saboor*?'

Omar wiped his hands on his *galabeya* before picking up Leila and swinging her round.

'It's a party for our baby daughter. When a baby is born, the parents have a party on the seventh day. We light candles and tell the child to listen to her mama and her papa and be an obedient child to God.'

'But Leila is six weeks old. And we don't have any plates or money to get anything for anyone,' I protested.

'This *saboor* must take place,' replied Omar. 'Mama and Papa will bring everything we need. It will be when Leila has been in Egypt for seven days. It will take place on Friday.'

'Without you? Omar, I'm not sure I'll be able to manage. Can't we postpone it?'

'I will be there, *habibti*. I will come back every week.' He pulled me to him and kissed me hard.

I clung to him, not wanting to let go. 'What time do you have to leave?' I whispered.

'I must go now,' he replied. 'Mohamed will drive me to Fayoum and my uniform is at Mama's.' He kissed me again. 'I will think of you always. I love you.'

'But where is Mohamed? Surely he has to come here to pick you up?' I said, wanting to delay his departure for as long as possible.

'Mohamed is already here,' he replied, 'talking to the men in the workshop downstairs. Remember to ask Tarek for anything you need.'

I felt very alone in the flat, knowing that I would be there for a week before Omar returned. When Leila fell asleep, I lay down on the lumpy mattress and cried all night.

I was very nervous about returning to work with a baby. George was there to pick me up in the morning. As we left the flat, I could feel several pairs of eyes watching me. I held Leila close and stared at the ground until I reached the top of the street where the minibus stood. I had forgotten to ask how I should behave with our neighbours and I didn't want to make any mistakes that might jeopardise me going out to work.

At school everyone welcomed us with open arms. Leila was instantly whisked away by two Egyptian ladies, who fussed over her, crying, 'Me'sha'allah'.

Even Mrs Sellar was interested in my journey home and the birth. It was obvious that they were genuinely glad to see me and I relaxed. I told them about Karen and swore them to secrecy.

'Now tell us about coming back to Egypt,' said Lisa. 'Are you living in your new flat, or have you got to put up with the old dragon?'

I laughed. 'No, we've moved, or should I say, I've moved.

Omar's been called up. Leila and I will be on our own for a few months.'

Judith's eyes lit up. 'Oh, good. We can expect a few party invitations, then?'

I looked down. 'It's not like that. In fact, it's not how you might imagine a new flat to be at all.' Then I burst into tears. Judith put her arms around me as I sobbed uncontrollably. 'The wife's family is supposed to provide the furniture, which means me. So there isn't anything in the flat. It's just a space. We haven't even got a bed. There isn't even any water in the taps. I've no idea how we'll manage.'

'Don't worry,' Judith said. 'We'll help as much as we can. Remember you always have us.'

My distress was short-lived. The children were delighted to see me back and overjoyed to meet Leila. Within minutes of entering the classroom, I was engrossed in the working day. One of the helpers brought Leila to me in the classroom and she lay contentedly in her baby-bouncer. If she needed feeding, I would leave the children with a helper to attend to her. I had been very apprehensive about teaching with my baby in the room with me, but that first day, things went without a hitch. The other teachers were supportive, which gave me more confidence.

As I waited for George to return from his first round of lifts home, Lisa and Judith brought me some posters.

'Here, Jacky. Put these on your walls. Brighten the place up a bit. I've even got some Blu-tack.' Judith held out the posters.

I wedged them down the side of Leila's bag. 'Thanks. It's a great start.' I smiled. 'At least I have a blank canvas to work with.'

Sticking the posters on the wall changed the whole atmosphere from drab to interesting. There was definitely a more homely feel about the place.

For tea, I heated up the *fool* and *tarmeyer* from the morning. I hadn't had time for breakfast. I ate my fill with bread and cucumbers and almost enjoyed it. Full of protein, it was certainly good for me, although I tried not to think of the many pairs of unwashed hands that had been involved in its preparation.

I settled Leila down and went to bed. I had managed to get through another day. But was that what it was all about? Getting through the days? Since our return, there had been nothing but stress between us. I had imagined a romantic, passionate reunion, but our material needs had taken priority and my feelings had had to take a back seat. I decided to show Omar how well I could manage, and make him proud of me when he came on Friday.

During the next few days, Uncle Hassan delivered the dressing-table and wardrobe. I was so excited. There were no coat hangers, but Lisa gave me some. It felt as if I was really starting to get somewhere when I saw our clothes hanging neatly on the rough wooden pole.

Together with Mervette, I ventured out to the *souk* in the next street early one morning before school. I threw a black veil over my head to be less conspicuous. Mervette haggled over the price of everything and saved a lot of money. I followed her example and bought lettuce and potatoes without help. Children noticed my fair skin and blonde hair under the thin veil and followed us. They were constantly trying to touch me and asking the time, 'Sea'kem?' Mervette shooed them away, 'Emshou', and they ran off laughing.

There was a little shop on the roadside between the souk and the flats. From there I bought feta cheese, a tin of corned beef, tomato puree in little tins and sugar. These were very cheap items, which I thought would last me for the week. I managed to use Arabic for all of the shopping without stumbling once.

Friday came at last. There was no school, but Mohamed arrived early with chairs on the back of a lorry. He instructed me to stay hidden in the bedroom with Leila, while men carried them up. The day passed in a flurry of deliveries. By lunchtime, Mama and Papa had descended on us with pans of food, cooked chickens, rice, salad and cakes. Crates of Coke and 7-Up followed, and Tarek brought a table and a black-and-white TV from his flat for the occasion.

As the preparations took over, I was virtually ignored. I felt in the way in my own home. At siesta time, the family trooped over to Mervette's flat, as I had nothing to lie down on. I was delighted. I carefully picked from the dishes of food so that no one would notice, until I was full. The chicken smelt good, and I prised the top off a bottle of Coke to wash it down.

Towards evening after siesta time, the family drifted back

in, now dressed up for a party with lavish make-up and hairdos. Magda looked stunning. She had been to the *coiffeuse* and her hair was drawn up away from her face, revealing delicate gold earrings. Her prospective husband had been invited and she was dressed to impress in an outfit made out of gold shimmery material, high-heeled gold shoes and gold bracelets on each wrist.

Relatives began to arrive, kissing me and sitting on the chairs around the edge of the room. Children ran around chasing one another. The women wore heavy make-up and brightly coloured turbans or veils. The men wore shirts and trousers and were dull in comparison. Most of them sported a black moustache to match their dark, bushy eyebrows. Abdel Menem, Magda's prospective husband, was tall with small, dark eyes. His hairline was receding, making him appear older than his years. As he came over to greet me, I decided he looked shifty. I offered my hand for him to take. I knew now not to shake his hand and not to expect him to shake mine. He took my hand gently in his and instantly withdrew it, as was the norm. I looked up to say good evening, and as I did so he smiled. His smile softened his appearance as his eyes crinkled at the edges and lit up with pleasure. He turned and went to sit beside Magda, stopping to say a few words to Mama on the way, who was delighted.

Tambours appeared and a few women began to beat out a rhythm to which everyone else clapped, intensifying the pulse. Candles were lit. I had no idea where they had come from, but it was plain that the occasion had very little to do with me anyway. Adults and children alike were given a lighted candle and the lights were switched off.

As people called for me to fetch Leila, the door opened and Omar appeared. There was no time to say hello. A candle was thrust into his hand and he went around the room greeting people. I picked up Leila and, as instructed, placed her carefully on a prayer mat in the middle of the floor. Salma knelt beside her with a huge mortar and pestle and began to bang it loudly, chanting things, to which everyone shouted replies. I didn't understand it all, but watched, fascinated, nevertheless. The next part was alarming. Everyone got up and formed a line with their lighted candles and stepped over Leila, while the tambours continued to beat their hypnotic rhythm together with the clanging of the mortar and pestle and the chanting voices.

I was sure that Leila would get her tiny face burnt with hot wax. I looked helplessly to Omar. He caught my eye, registered my concern, shook his head to reassure me and winked. It went on and on, the chanting almost hypnotic and suddenly, as if a message had been passed among them, they were silent. I was allowed to pick Leila up and take her into the privacy of Mervette's bedroom to feed her and the clapping began again.

The celebrations went on for several hours. Magda sat beside Abdel Menem, holding his hand, a permanent smile on her face. Papa had agreed to the marriage. She looked very pretty in her new dress and it was obvious Abdel Menem thought so too. I put Leila to sleep, but all the other children were still running around at eleven o'clock. Children didn't have bedtimes, but instead went to bed when their parents did. Celebrations always included the whole family, with the babies and children fitting in with the occasion.

Gradually the guests began to leave and by midnight they had all gone. Omar stacked the chairs in the sitting-room. Mama and Salma collected the empty plates, glasses and pans into a large box and Mohamed put the empty bottles into crates. Tarek took the table and television to his flat and I fetched Leila back to ours.

I was secretly pleased that the family had bothered with the *saboor*. They had made it clear that they had wanted a boy, and hadn't made that much of a fuss over Leila up until then. Even the teachers at the school had made more of her. It wasn't the end of the world, as Mervette already had Ahmed, but it made me feel that once again I had failed.

That night Omar and I slept together, abandoning the mattress in favour of one blanket on the floor and the other to cover us with. We made passionate love and after a quick wash from the bowl, slept with our arms tightly around one another. I had waited two whole weeks to hold him, to touch him, to be with him like this and he made everything better. Of course we would manage. I was full of renewed hope for the future.

The next morning, over *fool* and bread, Omar informed me that he had to leave early that afternoon and that we were eating with Mama. 'Remember to bring Leila's birth certificate. You should have shown it to Papa last night, but you were feeding her and then I forgot.'

At Papa's I gave Leila a good wash, had a shower and washed my hair. After eating, we gathered in the reception room in front of the television. I proudly unfolded the birth certificate and presented it to Papa, knowing it was the first time they would have seen one in English. Papa put on his glasses and examined it closely, holding it close to his face. He called Salma, and her smile faded as she scanned the document, obviously looking for something. There was a rapid conversation and Omar strode over, snatched the certificate and examined it himself. He read aloud slowly, 'Leila Anne.'

'I named her after my mother. It's a lovely idea, don't you think?' I smiled.

Omar, his face ashen, turned to me. 'You have named my daughter Leila Anne? Where is her father's name? Where is Leila Omar?' He was shouting now, his eyes flashing with anger. I was afraid. What had I done?

'She is a girl. Omar is a boy's name,' I faltered.

'You telephoned from England and we agreed that you call her Leila,' he bellowed. 'We told you that the baby's name would be Adham Omar Ibrahim. You said you understood. So what is this?' He threw the certificate onto the bed in disgust.

I was confused. 'But why would we give a boy's name to a girl?' I whispered.

'You have disobeyed me. I will not allow this.' Omar suddenly raised his hand and struck me hard across the face. I fell backwards against the television, my cheek numb and my eye throbbing. I sat there stunned, as the whole family erupted. Papa was standing up shouting. Omar was flinging his arms around and shouting back. Mama and Magda were screaming. Mohamed was holding on to Papa and Salma to Omar as if they were going to start fighting.

No one had so much as blinked when Omar struck me. No one rushed to see how I was. The tears streamed down my cheeks as I wiped a tiny trickle of blood from under my eye where he had scratched me.

Then, suddenly, Papa was bending down close to my face and shouting at me to leave. '*Emshi, emshi. Rooh she'ik.*'

Omar took Leila and we were bundled into a taxi. He was smouldering with rage all the way. I didn't dare utter a word. Inside the doorway he lifted his foot and kicked me hard in my back so that I lost my footing and went sprawling across the floor. He set Leila down into her bouncing chair, came over and pulled me to my feet. He shook me by the shoulders, asking me why, over and over again. '*Lay? Lay kedda? Lay Jacky? Lay?*'

Without another word, he collected his kit-bag and left, slamming the door behind him. I tried to examine my face in my handbag mirror. There was a nasty bruise around one eye, and the imprint of his hand on my cheek was plain to see. My face was smeared with dust, blood and tears. Gently I bathed it with some of Leila's cotton wool I had brought from England. I'd have to think of a good story to tell the girls at work. They mustn't know the truth.

I lay down to think through the events of the last hour more carefully. I had learned that it was the custom to give every child, regardless of their sex, the name of their father and then their grandfather. Once again, in my ignorance, I had displayed enormous disrespect towards the family.

No wonder they had been angry. I deserved everything I got. I felt so guilty, so embarrassed, so ashamed, so miserable. I was an awful wife. And now Omar had gone and there was no time for me to ask him to forgive me. How could I have been so stupid? I eventually dropped off to sleep wondering if I would ever be good enough to be accepted as part of the family. I determined to try even harder.

24

Survival

Gradually the family withdrew their support. Leila was not only a girl; she was a girl with an unacceptable name and a disrespectful mother. Mervette, though, was a great help, taking Leila for me while I whipped around cleaning the flat, doing bits of hand washing and boiling nappies. Every Friday, Omar would arrive and, instead of visiting Papa, we would wash each other's hair and sit on the tiny balcony with Leila, drinking tea and looking up at the stars.

He didn't mention the subject of Leila's name, and I was sensible enough to avoid it as well. After a long, sticky working week, I longed to be invited for a shower and a decent dinner to Papa's. I also missed Salma and her cheerful conversations. But I knew that this was another subject that I could not raise myself. I was out of favour, and only Papa could invite me back into the family fold.

Money, or lack of it, was becoming a serious issue. I had overlooked the need to tip the *bawab*, the man who lived in the doorway of the buildings, when he sent the man up with a new *embuba*, a gas bottle, for the Primus stove, or if he brought up a letter. I found it very difficult to understand his Arabic, as he mumbled his words and never looked directly at me. Every sentence sounded more like a growl, yet I was aware that he took care of me in his own way. I always made sure to thank him profusely for the jobs he did and give him a tip, no matter how hard up I was. Every piastre was precious and despite being as prudent as I could, my wages ran out a week before any more were due.

Christine and Elizabeth both gave private lessons in English to boost their incomes. I was tempted to speak to Omar about the idea, although I was not sure myself how I would manage this with a baby.

When Omar came home two weeks after the *saboor* and did not mention Papa, I gathered up the courage to broach the subject of home tuition. He listened carefully as I outlined the idea, leaning forward with interest. When I came to the part about how much I could earn, he began to smile and then swung me round delightedly.

'Jacky, this is a wonderful idea, a brainwave,' he said. 'You can give the lessons here in the flat. Of course you need a man here to protect you; a woman cannot receive strangers into her home when her husband is not there. Tarek will sit with you.'

He paced up and down the sitting-room area, his mind working overtime, his thoughts swinging from one thing to another in the same breath. 'You will need a table and two chairs. Maybe a rug. And on the days Tarek is working, Mohamed can come. Papa will forgive you when he sees how independent you are. And there will be more money, and you will be happier. Yes, this is a very good idea.'

*   *   *

It was simple to arrange. Mrs Sellar gave me two pupils to begin with, and was kind enough to supply me with the books I would need. George turned up and donated two chairs from the school. I would have loved to ask him in, but we both knew how inappropriate this would be, and he left them downstairs for the *bawab* to bring up, with a note wishing me good luck. Tarek brought the base of a table, made out of light aluminium. The workmen cut a circle of chipboard to balance on the top and Mervette presented me with a cloth to cover it. A large rectangle of brown rush matting completed the ensemble, and suddenly I had a dining-room.

My pupils were both delivered to the door by their *dadas*, or nannies, who arranged a pick-up time with me and scuttled down to the waiting *sooweh'*, the driver. Tarek would also greet them and sit in the bedroom reading his paper until the lesson was over. This was by no means a gesture of generosity on his behalf. He was a big lump of a man and in my opinion, still a spoilt little boy who liked his own way. It was no effort at all for him to lounge on the bed, drinking tea and reading the paper. It got him out of doing anything more strenuous elsewhere. On several occasions, he had brushed against me when entering the flat and immediately apologised. He didn't fool me for a minute; his actions had been intentional and we both knew it. Occasionally at Papa's, I would catch him leering surreptitiously over the top of his newspaper at my body, making me stiffen and make an excuse to leave the room.

The pupils were two girls, aged eight and ten. They were very well-behaved, and eager to learn. If Leila needed attention during the tuition hours, I would simply pick her up and rock her gently to comfort her.

I charged LE3 for the lessons. This made such a difference to the housekeeping. After the first week, Omar took me to see Papa and the family and proudly told them of my enterprise. They hugged me, kissed Leila, and offered me a shower. I had been forgiven. Papa even let Omar bring his old double bed to our flat. It was a luxury to have a bed in the bedroom, even if the mattress had seen better days. I slept like a log, waking each morning feeling refreshed, and gradually my spirits lifted.

Mrs Sellar approached me in her maternal way the following week and took my two hands in her own. 'You have made a good impression, Jacky. The parents discuss everything between them, you know, and word has gone round that you are a patient, understanding tutor. Could you possibly take on three more pupils, do you think?'

'I'd love to,' I replied. 'I'm sure I can fit them in. I thought it would be difficult to look after the baby at the same time, but I'm managing all right.'

I looked down at Leila, whose blue eyes had now changed into the deep brown of her father's, and tickled her under her chin. She gurgled and smiled in response, but then began to cough.

'That's a bad cough. She needs a doctor, Jacky,' Mrs Sellar

remarked, examining Leila's face. She was sweating and her little cheeks were bright red.

I looked at Leila in horror. Mrs Sellar was right. My heart sank and I began to panic. 'But I never leave the flat except to come to school or go to the market. I don't even know where a doctor is. What can I do?'

'George will take you to our doctor if you wish,' Mrs Sellar suggested. She laid her hand on my arm as if to calm me as I rocked Leila back and forth and considered her kind offer.

'No, thank you. I'll see how she is tonight and ask Mervette about a family doctor. I don't know if my father-in-law would approve of me taking her to another doctor and I can't risk upsetting him again.'

'If you're sure. The offer is always there. I'll delay your new pupils until Leila's well.' Mrs Sellar took the baby from me and loosened the blankets to give her some air. 'I'll ask *dada* Samia to stay with her this afternoon. It's probably not a good idea to have her beside you in the classroom like this.'

I smiled in gratitude, as she called for Samia to take Leila. Samia was a short, buxom lady, very black with a loud voice. She had a squint in one eye, so that when she spoke, it was difficult to know who she was looking at. She took Leila out of her bed, saying, '*Y'eyenna y'assal, mekoolsh? Mairlik enti, mairlik?*' Are you poorly, my sweet? Aren't you eating? What's wrong?

Through the day, Leila refused to breastfeed. She was sick, and I was very uncomfortable and sore as a result. At the flat, I rushed to ask Mervette's advice, but there was no one in. I couldn't believe it. She was always there, and the one time I really needed her, the place was in darkness. I knocked and called until my knuckles hurt, and in desperation laid my head on her front door and began to cry.

As I wiped my hair away from my face and turned back to my flat, I heard a sound above me. I looked up to see a woman on the stairs and a boy of about eleven standing behind her. She introduced her son as Youssef and herself as his mother, Om Youssef. Her head was uncovered, revealing long hair roughly pushed into a pony tail. It was black, although streaked with grey. Speaking loudly and slowly with grand gesticulations, she explained that they had moved into the flat above ours. She asked us to come in and see it.

I looked doubtful, and muttered, '*Fee ragil foh? Gozik?*' If her husband was in, there would be trouble and it was the last thing I wanted.

When I spoke in Arabic, her face lit up. '*Ti kelim arabi kwice. Enti zay masraya, hairlan. T'aaloh. Mafeesh ragil henna.*' Having complimented me on my Arabic, she reassured me that there was no man upstairs. She took Leila in her arms upstairs, leaving me to follow.

The inside of her flat was fascinating. A gilt-edged couch and two matching chairs made up the reception room. They had seen better days and were scratched and scuffed, the seats covered with prayer mats. A large gilt frame housing a portrait of President Anwar el Sadat hung precariously from a long nail on the wall. In the corner a black-and-white television stood on a table, with a filthy cassette player on the top of that. Both were switched on, making the sound jarring and indistinguishable.

Om Youssef ushered me in and made me sit on the couch with Youssef. She took Leila with her into the kitchen while she made *ahwa*, and presented it with a glass of water on a tarnished gilt tray.

I sipped the thick, sweet coffee, followed by gulps of water to dull the taste. Youssef got up and turned the volume of the television down, leaving the screen on. I listened to the sad wailing of the singer on the cassette. Leila was asleep. Om Youssef handed her back to me and brought out a thin, black cigarillo, which she lit up contentedly. She looked at me with tears in her eyes and nodded towards the cassette. '*Hellwa, mushkedda?*'

I nodded back, although to me the singing hadn't really improved even without the opposing voice of the television. Om Youssef loved the song and I would have insulted her had I disagreed. '*Hellwa awee,*' I replied, agreeing that the singing was beautiful.

'Om Kalsoum,' she whispered, closing her eyes and inhaling the strong smoke.

Om Kalsoum was the diva of all divas, respected un-reservedly by all Egyptians. She had been singing for years and with the backing of a full orchestra performed lavish concerts, which were televised weekly.

I complimented Om Youssef on her flat, knowing this was what I should say even if I really thought it was sad and rather tacky. Looking round, I could see that it was the home of a *baladi* family, as opposed to a more sophisticated one. Mervette's mother had provided Mervette with a beautiful sideboard and a dining table with chairs. For the *sarla*, the reception room, she had paid for moquette to be laid. This was a fitted carpet, rather than the traditional rugs, and was very modern. She had commissioned tradesmen to make a seven-piece suite in luxurious material edged with carved wood, which would be arriving soon. Mervette had ornaments and vases dotted around; her flat was enviable.

Om Youssef had old wooden boxes stacked up in one corner, tins of ghee piled up next to that and clothes hanging on a piece of rope strung across the room at the back. The shutters were open and bedding was piled over the windowsill to air.

I thanked her once again and got up to leave. She gave me some oil in a bottle that she told me to rub into Leila's chest.

At home, I watched anxiously over Leila. She took a feed towards evening, but coughed and whimpered all night. By morning she had developed a fever and I was frantic. I woke Mervette and she persuaded Tarek to contact Mohamed. I was unable to let George know, so he made the journey to take me to school for nothing. He could see how worried I was and I promised to call from Papa's to let him know what was happening. Mohamed drove us to Papa's. Mama was waiting on the doorstep, dressed in outdoor clothes. I didn't even get out of the car. Mama climbed in and we drove straight to the doctor's.

The surgery was busy; we waited in a long, whitewashed corridor lined with chairs. When our turn arrived, only Mama and I took Leila in to see the doctor. He shook Mama's hand lightly and spoke rapidly in incoherent Arabic, examining Leila at the same time. It was as if I was invisible. He lifted her nappy, rubbed her buttock with cotton wool and drove a syringe deeply into her skin. Three minutes later we were driving back to Mama's flat, having paid him a fortune for his advice, a supply of syringes, needles and medicine.

It was pointless asking Mama what he had done, so I did the sensible thing and stayed for the day with them, cleaning the flat and preparing vegetables in between caring for Leila. When Salma finally returned from college, she was able to explain that Leila had pneumonia. I would have to administer the injections myself three times a day for six days, and bathe her forehead with cool water regularly. Oh, and I owed Papa LE25.

Salma told me this in a very matter-of-fact way, as if it was quite normal to give your baby injections in her bottom. I felt quite dizzy with the responsibility and told her so. She merely giggled, showed me how to fill the syringe, release excess air, hold the buttock down between two fingers and inject with a firm, constant action, pulling it quickly out as soon as the medicine had gone into her body.

That evening I tried, but had to use the other buttock, as the left one was so red and sore. I managed, but Leila screamed for ages and made herself sick.

I telephoned George, finally getting through after forty minutes. He told me to take the week off; he would cancel my home pupils and pick me up the following Sunday. We slept at Papa's. It was lovely to spend time with Salma, feel the electric fan on my face and eat chicken.

In the morning, even though Leila had only woken once, I

felt really tired. My breasts were sore and when I tried to feed her, she couldn't get enough milk and cried. After sitting with her for an hour, Mama stormed in to see what was the matter. She saw that I wasn't producing much milk and sent Mohamed to the pharmacy to fetch some baby milk. Leila was fed and comfortable within ten minutes.

I felt useless. What was the matter with me? My back ached, my head was spinning and my milk was drying up. Mama came through to sit with me while Leila was still drinking from her bottle. Salma also joined us.

'It's very soon after Leila to have another baby. But it's God's will. This time, *inshahallah*, you will have a son,' she said.

'What are you talking about? I can't be pregnant.' I was indignant. 'Leila is only three months old. It's ludicrous.'

To cap it all, Omar was unable to get home that Friday. I returned to our flat, nursing Leila through her illness, sorting out the sterilising set for her bottles and buying SMA formula milk for her to drink. I had little time to consider the fact that I might be pregnant.

On Sunday, George picked us up as usual. Leila was faring much better on the bottle and although I had stabbed her in every bit of her tiny bottom, it had been for her own good and she was now on the mend. I gave her to Samia, who was delighted we were back, and rushed to find Judith.

'Oh God, Judith, I'm in such a mess. I'm broke, I already owe money to Papa, my milk's dried up and I think I'm pregnant again.'

'No, Jacky, you can't be.'

'That's just it. I have to be sure, but I can't afford it. Could you get me a home pregnancy kit at lunchtime? I'm desperate. Please?'

Judith smiled wryly. 'I'll do better than that. She went to the office to use the phone and arranged for her housekeeper to buy a kit there and then. 'There, that's settled,' she said, replacing the receiver. 'My driver should deliver it within the hour.'

I was pregnant. Again Christine, Judith, Elizabeth and Lisa were all supportive, but I was devastated.

'How did it happen? We haven't even got a bed, he's never here and we've only made love once or twice since Leila was born.' I put my head in my hands. 'We were just getting things straight, with the extra money from the lessons and the little bits for the flat. What on earth will we do now?'

Elizabeth answered me. 'You'll manage. Somehow.'

The next week I resumed the home tuition, taking on another girl and two boys. They were all charming. Tarek took it in turns with Om Youssef to sit in the flat; she had assumed a motherly role towards us and I was growing fond of her. During the times we sat together drinking *ahwa*, she told me that she did have a husband, but only for two days every fortnight. He had two other wives and he allocated specific days to live with each of them. He was not Youssef's father, so Om Youssef was the least popular of his wives. He had done her a big favour by offering to marry her, she had told me. She was grateful. On the day he was due, she made sure the flat was spotless, cooked a lot of food and wore her best clothes for him.

I was amazed that she was satisfied with such an arrangement, but she only laughed and said it was the best thing that could have happened. Her first husband had blown himself up in the kitchen of their old flat, when he had lit a cigarette and thrown the match onto the hose that connected the *embuba* to the cooker. The hose was old and perished, and gas was escaping through it. Youssef had been only two years old, and when her present husband had offered to marry her, she had jumped at the chance, in spite of his other wives and seven children. A woman without a husband in Egypt was virtually an outcast. She kept herself to herself and had grown accustomed to this new way of living.

Often, having drunk the *ahwa*, she would swirl the dregs around the cup and turn it upside down to read her fortune. Whenever she read my cup, she would see long roads indicating travel, and more children. She remained adamant that I would have three healthy children in my life, two girls and a boy.

After my first lesson with Hosni, a nine-year-old boy, his mother came up to the flat to speak to me. She was very wealthy, dressed in a modern, tailored suit and a smart, leather coat. Her hair was drawn up into a chignon and uncovered. She pressed five pounds into my hand, saying that I should charge LE5 for every hour, rather than only three. In future, she would send this amount for Hosni's lessons, she said. She thanked me, offered a limp handshake, and left.

The news spread quickly that Hosni's mother had visited my humble home, and the next day, the drivers of all my other pupils delivered the same message; they would be paying LE5 in future for their children's tuition.

It was Omar's birthday that Saturday. I had the money to cook a decent meal and the ingredients for a cake. Without an oven, I decided to tip Samia at school, who agreed to do it for me and produced a wonderful cake with a jam and custard filling.

'I'll feed him and tell him about the baby when he's relaxed and Leila is sleeping,' I decided. 'I hope he'll be pleased.'

The meal went well. Omar was attentive and desperate to make love, but I delayed him, fussing over Leila and staying with her until she slept. Eventually, I crept out of the bedroom, ready to tell him my news. If we made love, he would be in no mood afterwards to talk. I brought out the cake and he made tea, nuzzling my neck while I told him about the extra money that would be coming in from now on.

He sat down with his cake and pulled me onto his knee. '*Wahasteeni, habibti,*' he said, kissing me.

'I've missed you too,' I replied, removing his hand from my breast and sitting up to face him. 'I have another birthday present for you,' I continued. 'A surprise.'

'What is it?' He looked around, puzzled.

'We're going to have another baby.' I looked at him expectantly as he took in the full meaning of my words.

Suddenly he stood up, pushing me away from him and

flinging the cake on the floor. His eyes were flashing dangerously as he grasped my dress and hauled me to my feet until his face was close to mine.

'You are crazy. There can be no more babies now. We have no money, nothing in the house, no car, not even a fridge to make the water cold enough to drink. No, there will be no baby.'

He raised his fist and smashed it into the side of my face. I wasn't expecting him to hit me and was unprepared. The blow sent me right across the room, and I crashed against the shaky, make-do table, toppling it on top of me.

I sat up angrily, wiping the blood from my mouth with my sleeve. Rage surged through me as I stood up shakily.

'How dare you hit me? How dare you blame me for your carelessness?' I screamed. 'You think you're so strong when you hit me, don't you? Does it make you feel good? Well, I think it makes you look ridiculous. You're nothing but a bully.'

Seeing the cake on the floor, I bent down and scraped up a piece with my finger.

'Is it not *haram* to throw food away?' I asked him. 'Or do you ignore the rules of Islam when it suits you?'

I smeared the cake all over his face as he stood there, incredulous that I was speaking to him in such a way. I didn't care. I was hurting, inside and out. I had nothing left to care about. I turned away and slumped down on a chair. The pain from his blow had started to rush in, and my mouth was bleeding so badly I had to swallow the blood.

In a flash, Omar was at my side, dragging me up, kicking me in my back so that I fell down with a groan. He carried me into the bathroom where he used a beaker to pour water over my head, smearing the blood over my face and through my hair.

'No wife of mine ever speaks to me like that,' he snarled. 'I will not be questioned about Islam. You will be punished.'

He grabbed my hair with one hand and dragged me back into the reception room. The pain was dreadful, as if my ears were being ripped off. I began to sob. 'I'm sorry, Omar. Please stop, please.'

He turned me over and stamped hard four or five times on my stomach. I let out a terrible scream and was sick at the same time. I found the strength from somewhere to drag myself to my knees. Sick clung to strands of my hair and stuck to my face as I tried to stand up. I cried out as pain ripped through my stomach, but still I tried to run away.

At the door, he stopped me, closing his hand around my neck and squeezing. I struggled, but it was no good; he was far too strong. I couldn't breathe, my head felt as if it was going to burst, and then suddenly I felt my body going limp.

The last thought to rush through my mind was, 'He's going to kill me.'

With the last ounce of strength, I closed my eyes, raised both of my hands and scratched him hard, all the way down his throat, drawing thick lines of blood as I did so. With a roar, he let me go, grasping his neck and swearing.

I didn't need a second chance. In a flash, I had opened the front door and was pounding desperately on Mervette's door.

That evening, it was Mervette who saved my life.

25

Recriminations

Mervette took one look at me, pulled me inside and shut the door, bolting it firmly. '*Tarek, tarl henna shuf Jacky bisorra.*'

Tarek, who had been watching television with Ahmed and his mother-in-law, Mama Farida, jumped up to help carry me to their bedroom and lay me carefully on the bed. I curled up into a ball, holding my stomach and weeping. My mouth continued to bleed steadily. There was a lot of blood streaked over my face, neck and dress.

Mervette fetched some powdered coffee and smeared it into my lip to stem the bleeding. Tarek covered me with a blanket, as I was shaking. My stomach gave an involuntary heave and I retched again and again. Mervette helped me to sit up and Tarek rushed to bring a bowl. I brought up nothing but bile. Finally my stomach calmed and I was able to lie down again.

I hurt so badly I wanted to die. As the blanket warmed my body, I began to think beyond the pain to what had happened. I put out my hand to touch Mervette. '*Mervette, ana owse Leila, min fadlik haitili Leila dulwati.*' I needed Leila with me.

She nodded and sat with me on the bed, gently stroking my

cheek. Mama Farida looked on, frowning anxiously, holding little Ahmed's hand to prevent him climbing on the bed and disturbing me further. He was bewildered, his tearful, brown eyes full of confusion.

It was Tarek who went over to our flat. We could hear raised voices. Tarek was the eldest brother in the family and was pulling rank, telling Omar off for hurting me. There was a lot of swearing, the sound of a door banging, and then Tarek returned with Leila in her basket.

Omar began banging on the front door and shouting to be let in. I shrank back in fear, looking at both Tarek and Mervette imploringly. It was Mama Farida who took charge of the situation. She told Tarek to go and calm Omar down. She suggested he take him to Papa's for the night while she cared for us.

I must have looked in a sorry state, because Tarek agreed immediately, even asking the *bawab* to hail a taxi to take them. We waited there on the bed for what seemed like hours. It was actually no more than ten minutes before a taxi arrived and took both men away.

Mama Farida put some water on the cooker to boil, shooed Ahmed away and turned her attention to me. I watched as she examined my face, tutting all the while. She was a tall, handsome woman in her fifties with strong features, who took great care with her appearance. She gently cleaned away the dried sick mixed with blood and said she would wash my hair. I could only nod; the pain prevented me from speaking, and I couldn't manage a smile.

Mervette went to my flat and fetched nappies, bottles and

milk for Leila and a *galabeya* for me. She had only just returned when there was a loud rap at the door. I froze.

It was Om Youssef. She had heard the commotion and wanted to help. Mama Farida immediately handed Leila to her. Ahmed was also sent upstairs to play with Youssef.

Mama Farida then dabbed iodine on my cuts and helped me change my bloody dress for the fresh *galabeya*. She gasped when she saw my stomach. There was a wide area of deep red, some of which was darkening into a reddish purple.

She stroked my head, saying, '*Naym, yaroohi, naym,*' sleep, darling, sleep.

Safe for the time being, knowing Leila was in good hands, I could allow myself to drift off to sleep. It was a blissful relief from the dull pain that racked my stomach.

Several hours later, I was awoken by Mervette, who urged me to drink some warm tea. As soon as I opened my eyes, the pain was there again, stabbing now. I was stiff and had difficulty sitting up. I sipped the tea. Mama Farida appeared with a worried smile. She looked meaningfully at Mervette, who then told me that Papa was on his way back with Tarek and Omar. He would make sure that I would not be hurt any more and I was not to worry. I nodded, but was secretly terrified.

When the men arrived, Mervette stayed with me in the bedroom, locking the door, while we listened to the conversation outside in the reception. Omar came right up to the door and spoke in a soft voice, imploring me to come out. He promised not to hurt me again.

I swung my legs over the end of the bed, grimacing in pain

as I gingerly stood, leaning on Mervette. I waited at the door, listening to him pleading, a thousand thoughts racing through my mind. Eventually, I opened the door.

As I stepped over the threshold, Omar grabbed my arm forcefully and yanked me into the centre of the room. With a cry, I crumpled into a heap. I looked up to see Omar towering over me, his fist clenched.

There was a commotion. Papa roared, Tarek leapt upon Omar to restrain him and they began to fight each other.

I suddenly felt very dizzy. Seconds before passing out, I heard Mervette's piercing scream and then silence.

I opened my eyes to see Om Youssef, bathing my forehead and crooning softly. Mama, Salma and Magda were in the room, talking together in hushed tones. The television was still on in the background. I was lying on a sheet on a couch in Mervette's flat. The men had disappeared.

Mama Farida appeared with towels and damp rags. She knelt down in front of me and gently opened my legs. I looked down and stared.

Mervette stifled a sob as her mother mopped up the blood. No one uttered a word. Maybe two hours passed, and I felt a different sort of pain, a more urgent kind. I shouted for Salma, who held me while I pushed, not very hard, as I felt an involuntary spasm pass through me.

It was over very quickly. I pushed the tiny foetus out onto a towel. Blood red, only the size of a tomato, it was nevertheless clear to see that it was a boy.

Mama Farida took hold of the umbilical cord, as thin as cotton thread, and gently drew out the afterbirth.

Om Youssef raised her head and screamed out her distress. She put her hand to her mouth and continued to wail, 'Oweeeeeeeeeeeeeeeee.'

Everyone began to cry. I turned my head to the wall, as if to disassociate myself with their noise. I felt numb.

Omar returned to the army without a word to me. I was taken to Papa's, where I busied myself with looking after Leila. The family made no demands on me. Mama made me her special drink, very sickly, which she assured me would build up my strength.

I wrote my weekly letter home, full of entertaining stories about school and Leila. News reached the school that I had miscarried and George called round, bearing flowers, fruit and good wishes from the staff. He didn't come in to see me, but gave everything to Mohamed at the door.

Three days later, I was able to walk around. I asked to return to my flat and telephoned George to say I was ready to receive my pupils at home.

Once again, they arrived with their *dadas* for lessons. The *dadas* brought beautiful gifts for me, ornaments and flowers. One mother had sent a basket of apples. Apples were so expensive that I had never eaten one in Egypt.

Judith and Lisa visited me at home for the first time. They looked so out of place. Judith was dressed in white linen trousers with a wide belt and a bright red T-shirt. Lisa wore a flimsy, silk summer dress in cornflower blue with a floppy hat. They wore high-heeled strappy sandals, which highlighted their long, tanned legs.

At first they didn't notice the condition of the flat. They were shocked to see my bruised, swollen face. Judith rushed up to me. 'Oh my God, what happened to you? We knew you'd lost the baby, but this is something else.'

'I slipped washing the floors, hit my face on the side of the table and that's how I lost the baby,' I said, although I'm sure they knew I was lying.

They then turned their attention to the flat, wandering round, looking in each room with horror.

'Close your mouth, Lisa, or you'll catch flies.' I laughed for the first time since that dreadful day.

'Jacky, this is a hovel. How can you survive like this? You have nothing here. I must throw away things you could make good use of.'

'Let me make some tea,' Judith suggested, walking through to the tiny kitchen. She came straight back. 'Lisa, she hasn't even got a cooker, for God's sake. You've got one in your yard. You could get it here for her today. What do you say, Jacky?'

I looked at her, smiling. 'I say yes. Thanks a lot.'

The cooker arrived on a lorry a few hours later. The *bawab* and his wife carried it into the kitchen. His wife, a wizened little woman, possessed the strength of the devil. She returned later with a huge *embuba* on her head, which she placed next to the cooker. She held out her hand, muttering '*Gnay.*'

I fetched LE1 and pressed it into her hand, and then added ten piastres for herself. She shuffled out, leaving behind the scent of garlic.

One week previously, I would have hesitated when offered a gift such as a cooker, anxious that it might upset someone in the family. Now, I had been offered something that we needed for free and I was happy to accept it to make my life easier. It was a dull yellow in colour. There were four burners and an oven. Inside the oven, I discovered five oven trays. There was also a large drawer section at the bottom. It was like Aladdin's cave, full to the brim with saucepans.

Overcome with gratitude, I sat on the floor, rocking Leila back and forth and burst into tears. I cried for the kindness of my friends, for the concern of my Egyptian family, for the cruelty of my husband and finally, for the loss of our child.

After a while, I stood up and lit the gas on one of the burners to heat water for Leila's bottle in one of the saucepans.

I examined the gas bottle. It stood as tall as the cooker itself and was very heavy. Yet the tiny wife of the bawab had carried it in on her head, supporting it only with one hand. She had placed a piece of folded sacking between her head and the bottle and that was it.

As I waited for the water to boil, I let my mind wander to the next day, when Omar would be returning. I had not let myself think of him until now. I decided to take Leila to Papa's, where I would feel safer.

* * *

That evening, I packed a little bag with Leila's things and left the flat to take a taxi to Papa's. I had never ventured out alone like this before. As we left the building, I greeted the *bawab* and told him where we were going. I walked to the top of the street to wait for a taxi.

The night air was cool and refreshing. A wedding procession came round the corner and turned into our street. The bride and groom walked in the midst of guests, children and dancers, to the rhythm of tambours and wails from the women. The whole street was suddenly alive with colour, noise and excitement.

It was Thursday, the day when most weddings took place, a tradition probably started because the following day was a holiday. A taxi stopped for us, and we left the happy atmosphere, joining the dust and horns of the evening traffic.

Arriving at Papa's, I calmly paid the driver as if I did this sort of thing every day. Salma was delighted when I told her that I'd just got up and come.

Omar arrived the following day. I was preparing dinner with Mama in the kitchen, and he went in the bedroom to speak to Papa. We ate together as a family, and only then did Salma take Leila, leaving us alone.

I said nothing, making no attempt to touch him, sitting on the bed and waiting.

He sat beside me and stroked the back of my hand. Then he buried his head into my lap and began to sob. He told me how much he loved me, more than life itself. How hard he was going to work to make a good life for us. How desperate he had felt when I told him I was pregnant. How sorry he was for hurting the person he loved most in the world. Could I ever forgive him?

He rambled on and on. I hadn't expected a reaction like this. I had prepared myself to suffer harsh words, recriminations or rejection. My resolve to be apathetic and not react began to dissolve as I listened to his pleading. I reached out to stroke the top of his head. He looked up and I gazed deep into his brown eyes, now wet with tears, feeling that familiar rush of love envelop me. And I forgave him.

From that moment, Omar was very careful to put me first. He even wrote letters and brought them with him each week for me to read when he was away. He had been pleased about the cooker and also that I had used a taxi to get to Papa's. Life between us and in general improved. After a couple of months, my stomach was back to normal, although no one had suggested I visit the doctor. It didn't hurt any more and the bruising had gone, so I assumed everything was okay.

The summer drew on, bringing with it the unbearable midday heat. Lisa sent me two fans for the flat. Leila was a joy, both to me and to the staff at school. The family didn't fuss over her; Ahmed received all the attention, but she had enough from other people, so she didn't notice.

School finished, as did my home tuition for the summer. It was sad saying goodbye to everyone, although we would see each other in September. Much of my time was taken up in the company of Mervette and Ahmed, or Om Youssef. My knowledge and understanding of Arabic improved rapidly, so that I was able to disagree and question them quite naturally.

On the last day of August, I received a letter from home with the news that my parents were coming out for a visit in October, when Leila would be one. I was so happy at the thought of seeing them. On the same day, Omar returned from the army. He had completed his military service. He was home for good.

26

Culture Shock

Something inside me had died. The rush of emotion in the pit of my stomach whenever I thought of Omar had completely disappeared. Without school or home tuition, there was little stimulus for me to engage in flippant conversations or have a laugh to provide light relief from the drudgery of life in the flat. Omar left each morning to work for his father, leaving the day stretching ahead for Leila and me. On his return, he expected me to have a bowl of water ready so that I could wash his feet before his prayers.

Ramadan fell in the summer that year. Mervette explained that all Moslems fasted during the holy month of Ramadan to remind them how hard life was for poor people and to show respect to the teachings of the Koran. Hunger is the same for everyone, rich or poor, so the process makes everyone equal and able to concentrate on their religion.

This sounded all very honourable to me, until I was told that this fasting only went on during the daylight hours. To me this was the ultimate hypocrisy and a farce. It would have seemed more acceptable if people fasted in the day and then slept at night, but instead the women spent the days preparing gastronomic delights to gorge on when the sun went down.

These were my private opinions; conclusions I drew from first-hand experience of my family's perception of Islam and being a good Moslem. These thoughts remained private. I learned not to tell even my European friends anything that might be construed as controversial; it would eventually get out and undoubtedly be used against me. I had a daughter to protect as well now, and needed to be extra vigilant to avoid any aggressive confrontations.

Fasting was defined as abstinence from food, drink, smoking and sex – during the hours of daylight. Children were excused, as were the elderly, the sick, pregnant women and those who had their monthly period. Papa was therefore permitted morally to take his medication with water; Magda had a month-long period; two or three days into the fast, Mama would discover a dreadful ailment that required her to sip water throughout the day and the children obviously needed their food and drink.

Omar and his brothers stopped drinking beer throughout Ramadan, even in the evenings, but they all lit up as soon as they had finished eating. Special drinks were prepared: *tamarahind* was a liquorice drink that I particularly enjoyed. We made large jugs of it, using sticks of wood, which were actually liquorice sticks, waited for the initial call to prayer as the sun went down, and broke the fast with one or two glasses each.

Then we would gather round the feast, spread out in pans on newspaper on the floor, and stuff ourselves silly. It was quite ludicrous behaviour to an outsider, yet to the family these were gravely pious actions, which demonstrated their devotion to Islam.

Throughout the evening, the family would snack on this biscuit or that pastry, and finally retire around midnight. Around two-thirty in the morning, we would be awoken by a man walking up and down the streets ringing a bell and calling people to get up for the last meal. The family actually got up, heated rice, vegetables and meat, and had another meal before the day's fast, or *sawm*, began again at dawn.

As I was living within a Moslem community, I decided it would be both easier and respectful for me to fast as well. This simple action was looked upon very favourably, by the extended family as well, and Omar was very proud to tell them how well I could cook the *adds* (lentils) and *mollogheya*, or *samak* (fish).

At the end of Ramadan, the festival *Eed el Fetoor* took place. Papa gave *zakat*, bonuses, to his workers. This was a tradition based on the idea that everyone should have enough money to celebrate the feast, no matter how poor they are.

In the streets, special wooden scaffolding was erected, swathed in patterned red material, and vendors set up stalls selling sugary cakes, syrupy puddings, nougat with nuts inside and other sweetmeats. One of my favourites that I had now grown to like was *baclava*, flaky pastry with syrup and sugar, sickly sweet but delicious.

It was also traditional to buy new clothes and give small presents. The atmosphere in the streets changed dramatically, as people turned out in droves to celebrate, strolling up and down in high spirits. Mohamed drove the family to the zoo for a couple of hours. I walked around, bewitched by the atmosphere. It was crowded as people flocked to spend the day there, sitting on blankets on the grass in their hordes. There were balloons everywhere and children running happily around. There were little sideshows, and dancers, and brightly coloured hats and balloons on sale.

We saw a lot of the extended family and spent the evenings together at one another's homes, singing, dancing, clapping, eating and having a good time. The *Eed* celebrations continued for a week and were followed closely by another festival, *Eed el Adha*. As I was living at the flat, Mervette was my main source of information at the time, and she said we would be going out to Papa's workshop in a nearby village for another celebration the following week. There were palm trees along the road, villagers carrying huge loads on carts pulled by camels and children running alongside.

We all piled out of the white Peugeot to watch some men restraining a cow outside the main doors of the workshop. They then slit its throat and hung it up to let the blood drain out of its body. This was another rule of Islam: the meat eaten by Moslems had to be *halal*, allowed. To be *halal*, it had to be killed in this way. The workers scooped up blood as it gushed horribly from the dead animal's neck and smeared it on their foreheads. They approached Ahmed and Leila and did the same to them. I was horrified.

Mervette reassured me that this was a good thing, a tradition; Papa was sacrificing an animal as Ibrahim had prepared to sacrifice his son for Allah in the Koran. At the last minute, Allah had provided a ram for sacrifice instead. It was a symbol that Papa was ready to give up everything for Allah.

As the blood drained out of the cow, the men prepared a fire, while women fanned the flames with huge maize or banana leaves. The meat was stripped off the carcass and cooked immediately. The women put it between pieces of bread and distributed it among the villagers who were crowding round, eager for a share. Mama supervised some women to put some away in a plastic container she had brought with her; this turned out to be the family's share, which we enjoyed back at the flat with warm bread, salad and *salsa*, tomato puree.

I felt as if this was a new start for me as far as the family was concerned. Washing up at Papa's with Mama, she smiled kindly at me, saying, '*Enti zay masraya besoppt,*' you are exactly like an Egyptian.

September came, bringing with it a new term at school. Mrs Sellar welcomed us all back with some exciting news. She had successfully negotiated a deal to purchase new premises for the school and they would be moving in the New Year.

I realised that this would be a year of changes. Judith and Lisa would both be returning to England in January when their husbands' contracts finished. Christine, Elizabeth and Aisha all lived reasonable distances from the new location and I was the only one out in the sticks, so to speak.

Mrs Sellar called me into her office and explained that it would be too far for George to continue to pick me up after the move. There was a new English school being built near to the pyramids that would need English staff. She offered to contact the head and put in a word for me. I could only agree and concentrate on enjoying the last few months I had with the children I loved and the good friends I had made.

My parents were due at the end of the month. I was so excited. Our bed was finally finished and installed, so that we could offer the old one to Mum and Dad. Uncle Hassan gave us an old fridge, which made such a difference to us. Huge and cumbersome, it did the job it had been made for and at last we could have cold water to drink. I managed to get over twenty Coke bottles filled with water into the door of the fridge. It was pure luxury.

Omar was attentive and loving around me, and I was very careful not to upset him to spoil things. The day before my parents were due, he turned up at the flat with a disgustingly filthy, fraying three-piece suite, which he proudly installed in the reception. Straw was literally falling out of the ripped, faded velvet and it stank. I remained tactfully silent.

When we borrowed the Peugeot to collect my parents from the airport at 4 a.m., Omar was fidgeting nervously. He was eager to make a good impression and wanted so much for Mum and Dad to approve of him.

At the airport, things went well. After many hugs, kisses, tears and introductions, we were on the road heading for the flat. Leila went straight to my parents, which was unusual, as she had reached the stage of crying in front of strangers. Mum was delighted.

'Oh Jacky, she's adorable. Tell me everything about her, the words she knows and the things she can do.'

'Well, she doesn't respond very well to English, Mum,' I replied. 'I only speak Arabic to her, as that's what the family want.'

'How bloody ridiculous!' my dad exclaimed. 'The kid's surrounded by two languages and she's only learning one of them. I've never heard anything so bloody daft.' Dad, opinionated as ever, tutted and frowned.

'Sssh. Don't upset the apple cart. We've only just got here.' Mum tried to ease the tension in the air. We stared out of the window into the darkness.

I did my best to prepare them for the state of the flat. In my letters, I had focused on the positive things and created a false impression. Now they would see the reality.

Stepping from the car into the street, Mum carried Leila proudly into the building. Dad, however, stood and stared around him. Dawn was breaking, and with the light came the sight of a primitive street, muddy underfoot, and ground-floor flats without windows. Inquisitive children, barefoot, with grubby faces, peered at him from the dark recesses of doorways without doors. Without a word, he followed us up the steps to our flat.

'Welcome to our home,' Omar said, smiling.

'Sweet Jesus! This is what you've left England for?' Dad wandered slowly round, shaking his head.

Embarrassed at his rudeness, I turned desperately to Mum. 'We haven't had a chance to get ourselves on our feet yet. But now Omar's finished his military service and I'm working, we'll soon be able to afford nice things. Let me show you your room.'

Mum followed me into the second bedroom. I had pushed our old bed into one corner and stuck a poster of Winnie the Pooh on the wall. I had even borrowed sheets from Mama, so that they had a bottom and top sheet, with a blanket. But it was normal for them to have sheets on the bed, so the effort I had gone to went unnoticed. Mum turned to me, a tear running down her cheek. I wiped it away.

'Don't be sad, Mum. This is the life I've chosen. It's fine.'

'How can you live here, Jacky? Are you sure this building is safe? Have you seen the bricks on the outside? It has been built so crudely. And what about Omar? Are you happy together?'

'Yes, Mum. Now come and have some tea. Oh, and try to shut Dad up, will you? He's embarrassing me.'

The visit went from bad to worse. Everything shocked them, from the state of Papa's flat and their eating from saucepans on the floor, to the poverty that surrounded us in our flat. Mum was distraught at the prospect of surviving three weeks without a bath, let alone not having water in the taps, and within two days Dad had caught the runs.

'They should have booked into a hotel. This is too much for them to take in,' I whispered to Omar on the third evening, as Dad lay on his bed in between visits to the toilet, which of course didn't flush.

'Let's take them to lots of nice places. Then they have to

enjoy themselves,' he replied. 'I'll try and arrange a trip to Alexandria and Port Said.'

We tried everything. We spent a day in Alexandria, renting deckchairs and sitting on the beach. Leila had never been in the sea before. Among the many clothes and toys that Mum had brought with her for Leila was a little swimsuit. We put it on her and I paddled in the shallows, swinging her in and out of the water. She loved it. Mum and Dad took her in deeper and they both relaxed as the day progressed. They attracted lots of unwelcome attention, however, from leery men looking at Mum in her costume, so that she had to come out after a short while. All the other women went into the water with their clothes on and even their veils if they wore them.

In the evening, Dad felt well enough to take us out to eat at Shepherds Hotel. What a treat! He was in a better mood, and made pleasant conversation. By now, Omar's English was good enough to get by without anyone feeling uncomfortable. It was a magical evening, culminating in a stroll along the Nile watching the feluccas drift peacefully by.

Over the next week, we took them to the zoo, to Khanin Khalili, the flea market, Betty's tea shop in the city, the pyramids, with the sound and light show, and even up to Suez. This was new to me and I was surprised at how undeveloped it was. A sandy road led up to the canal and there were two restaurants at the end. We sat at one of the tables outside with umbrellas made out of branches and looked out onto the canal. There was a wall about chest height that you could sit on, and that was it.

We returned to Papa's, where Mama had said she would cook for us. Strangely, the street was unusually quiet and the shops had their shutters pulled down.

Inside Papa's flat, the television was on, a picture of the Koran on the screen, with someone chanting *suras* in monotone. President Anwar el Sadat had been assassinated at Victory Parade. This was a terrible shock and a tragedy. At the head of the Arab world, this man had held Egypt together and brought about so many liberating reforms.

We ate silently, sadly, with the drone of the television in the background. Finally a man appeared on the screen, informing us that the president was to be buried that Saturday. The new president to be sworn in would be Hosni Mubarek.

The remaining days of Mum and Dad's holiday dragged interminably. Dad couldn't shake off the runs, every public place closed out of respect for the president, and I had to return to school, as they would only give me one week off. Suddenly the streets were full of soldiers with guns and armoured cars.

Mum and Dad hated Egypt: the poverty, the dust, dirt and mosquitoes. I had hoped to convince them that I was really happy, so the rest didn't matter. But the rest did matter. It terrified both of them, and the assassination made them fear for our futures. Dad had a word with me in private about it. He sat with me on his bed and took both of my hands in his.

'Come back with us, Jacky,' he pleaded. 'We can't bear to think of you here after we're gone. Take Leila and come with us,' he repeated, more urgently.

'It's been a bit of a culture shock, I know . . .' I began.

'Culture shock,' he interrupted. 'You bet. This country is filthy, dusty, loud, poverty-stricken and disease-ridden and my daughter is living in conditions I have only ever seen in films, for God's sake. Yes, you may well say culture shock.'

I didn't tell him about the baby I'd lost. I didn't tell him how mixed up I was feeling. Part of me wanted to rush home to England without looking back. But there was still another part that wanted to make a go of things, despite what had happened in the past. I couldn't leave. Not yet.

27

Scum

The symptoms returned; by now they were recognisable. I no longer needed the confirmation of a test. I was pregnant again.

At school I sat with my head in my hands as I told Lisa my news.

'What's the matter, Jacky? Is it too soon? How do you feel? You don't look very happy about it.'

'Between you and me, I'm terrified,' I replied quietly. 'I don't mind having another child. In fact, after losing the last one, I'd be delighted. No, I'm worried about afterwards, how our family life will work out.'

'Whatever do you mean?'

I turned to look directly at her. 'Lisa, look at me. I've been here for nearly two years. Twenty-three months, to be precise. I've already given birth to one child, lost a child and I'm now on to my third. What the hell will things be like in ten years' time? I can see us with a whole football team.'

She looked at me, puzzled. 'You mean, you don't use contraception? But that's ridiculous. You have no control over your life. Jacky, you need to sort this out and quickly.'

*   *   *

I decided to tell Omar about the pregnancy in front of the family on Friday. Fortunately for me, they were delighted. They had other things on their minds. Magda was getting married to Abdel Menem in two weeks and Mama was in the midst of the preparations.

At home, I asked Mervette if she used contraception, as so far she had only her son, Ahmed. She said the doctor had fitted her with the coil. I stored away this vital piece of information for future use.

I arrived home from school the next day to find our little street crowded. Men and women were gathered outside a building a little further up, shouting across each other, making a huge noise. I hurried up to the flat, meeting Om Youssef on her way down.

'Ahlan, Jacky. Ana gaya dulwaty ekhod ho'ner.'

She kissed me on both cheeks and continued down the steps, without waiting for a reply. Injection? Why would she be going for an injection? I knocked on Mervette's door to find out.

There was cholera in the country. Mervette was preparing to take Ahmed and go for injections. She offered to take us as well.

In Arabic, I asked her, 'Is it very important?'

She stopped helping Ahmed with his coat, her face suddenly serious. 'It is a terrible illness, Jacky. We must all have the injection as soon as possible.'

'Is that why all those people are gathered downstairs?' I asked.

She smiled. 'The old man in the bottom flat always gives the injections for things like this. We will visit him now. Make sure your head is completely covered. Come.'

We made our way down the dark stairway and out into the blinding sunlight.

'Do you have money?' Mervette whispered.

'Some – why?'

'A good tip will get us in straightaway.'

I pushed fifty piastres into her hand. Within two minutes, a young man dressed in old trousers and a stained shirt ushered us into the building.

The room was dark, lit only by three candles. The mud floor was covered with thin, woven rugs. There was a bed in one corner. A very old, wizened man was sitting cross-legged on a blanket. He was dressed in a long, striped *galabeya*, with a white cloth draped round his head. There was a large box of sterilised needles in packets to one side. Next to that were the capsules of the vaccine. They looked totally out of place in such a primitive environment

I stood in the entrance, transfixed. Mervette nudged me back to life. 'You must pay him well, or we will all get the same needle.'

Stunned at this new piece of information, I pulled out a pound note, and then added another one, just to be sure. It was everything I had left for the week, but at that moment it seemed like value for money. He pocketed the money with a nod and indicated for us to sit. Mervette asked for four needles. We knelt in front of him and one by one, he swabbed our arms, filled the needles and injected the vaccine swiftly, using a fresh needle for each of us. Leila cried, but only for a minute. Ahmed screamed and kicked, which frightened Leila, so she started crying again. Having entered quietly, we were now attracting a lot of attention, carrying two screaming children.

Other children waiting outside surged towards us, touching me and shouting questions, asking my name, the time, if I was from America and so on. We battled through the crowds, reaching our building at last and fairly running up the steps.

So far in her little life, Leila had endured many injections. The doctor had administered some sort of triple vaccine called MMR when she was four months old. He said it was the latest thing and very safe so I believed him. After all the jabs I had given her when she was ill, she was used to them. She didn't make half as much fuss about them as Ahmed, who acted like a real wimp.

That Thursday, Magda was to be married. After school, George dropped me off at Papa's to help. The double doors leading from the reception to the front bedroom had been opened, the furniture pushed against the walls and chairs set around the edge.

The men brought cases of beer, a bubble pipe and hashish and took them into the back bedroom. The reception room was transformed. Chairs were placed around the room with two larger chairs at one end for the bride and groom, with a huge decoration made of leaves, flowers and ribbons standing between them.

Leila wasn't well. She had a bad cough, wouldn't eat and slept fitfully. I cuddled her, carrying her over my shoulder as I helped with the preparations.

Towards evening, the celebrations began. Magda looked radiant in a beautiful white wedding dress. She sat with Abdel Menem in the two chairs to receive the good wishes from all the guests. There was food, music and two belly-dancers.

Leila's condition worsened. She needed to sleep but the noise disturbed her. I decided to ask Omar if I could take her home. Mama agreed she needed quiet and gave me some medicine for her. Mohamed drove. Tarek came too, saying that he had forgotten the camera.

I knew they had been in the back room drinking beer and smoking hashish. Both brothers were in high spirits, making crude jokes and laughing loudly.

Mohamed took Leila from me and carried her up the stairs up to the flat. He then followed Tarek into his flat. I busied myself with Leila, changing her nappy, giving her a bottle and some of the medicine. She eventually dropped off to sleep. I tiptoed out of her bedroom and threw myself onto our bed, exhausted.

The room was in darkness. I lay listening for Leila, but all was quiet. I stood up to change. As I pulled my dress over my head, I heard a chuckle. I froze and stood very still, listening. Was Leila coughing? I'd change and then go and see her, I decided. I unhooked my bra and threw it down on the bed, reaching for a *galabeya* on the chair.

There was a hiccup and a hand reached out from the chair and grabbed my arm. I screamed, as Tarek forced my arm behind my back and manoeuvred me onto the bed.

'Mohammed! Mohammed!' I screamed. '*Sayidnee!*'

Tarek was a big man. With a cruel laugh he lay heavily on top of me, forcing my legs apart and fumbling with his flies. I threw my head from side to side, crying and protesting in vain.

Suddenly the light snapped on and Mohammed appeared. 'Thank you, God,' I prayed silently.

Mohammed was very drunk. He slumped down onto the chair, grinning horribly, watching his brother stuff his penis roughly inside his sister-in law as she writhed, screamed and begged him to help her.

Tarek gave a thrust, once, twice, and with a grunt relaxed his grip and rolled off the bed. I immediately sprang up, grabbing a *galabeya* to cover myself, and began shouting, shaking Mohammed to get Papa. Mohammed stared vacantly up at me.

Tarek straightened his shirt and left, pulling Mohammed after him. I ran to the top of the stairs, delirious with rage and shouted after them, 'You'll pay for this, you scum. You'll pay for this.'

I used all the water in the plastic bowl to wash away all traces of what he'd done. Omar would be angry. I didn't care. Leila was still sleeping. I sat on my bed in the dark, waiting for Omar to return.

He let himself in quietly about an hour later. I heard him go to the bathroom and swear when he found the water bowl

empty. He came into the bedroom and switched on the light
to ask me about the water. The question died on his lips as he
looked at my tear-stained face.

'What is it? Is it Leila?' he asked.

I shook my head miserably, looked directly into his eyes and
told him exactly what happened. I watched his eyes change and
harden as he took in my words.

And then he was hitting me, punches to my face and body,
shouting and swearing like a madman. I crumpled onto the
floor in a heap, shielding my stomach from him as he hit me
again and again. Then, with a final kick he left, slamming the
door behind him.

I waited there on the floor, straining to hear the sound of
him speaking to the *bawab*. Then I could be sure he had really
gone. Shakily I got to my feet. Pain seared through my left side,
so that I had to bend over to avoid crying out. I had to walk
bent double to the bathroom, only to remember that I had
used up all the water. I could see in the mirror that my face was
a mess, scratched and swollen, although not bleeding badly.

Moving awkwardly, I flung a few things into a bag with my
passport and all the money we had. Then I went to get Leila. I
was leaving. She was heavy and the pain in my side was intense.
I left the flat, but took ages to get down the steps, each one
causing me to grit my teeth to prevent calling out in pain.

It was a long journey to the bottom of the stairs. My
face streaked with sweat and tears, I struggled to the top of
the street with the intention of hailing a taxi. As I waited
desperately, Leila stirred in her sleep and fidgeted on my

shoulder, kicking me in the side as she did so. With a groan, the pain overrode all my senses and I could feel myself falling . . .

I woke up to a lot of shouting and noise. I was hurting badly and cried out as someone lifted me up. I could feel myself being carried up some stairs.

'No, no,' I shouted in horror. 'Don't take me back there.'

But no one understood. I thought I was being carried up to our flat, but we went past it and ended up in Om Youssef's flat. I was laid gently on her bed.

Om Youssef appeared holding Leila, looking very concerned. She settled Leila down and sat quietly, listening to my ramblings as I told her that Omar had hit me and I needed to leave now. I had difficulty breathing, which made talking hard and I had to bend over all the time. She bathed my face and covered me with a blanket. All I could say, over and over, was that I had to get out.

I stayed there for the rest of the night. In the morning, Omar visited. Om Youssef had no right to refuse him entry, so he walked right in and demanded that I return home. By this time, I could hardly breathe. I was rasping badly and couldn't move. I could hear them speaking in hushed tones and Omar left.

Later, he returned and carried me to the car where Mama and Salma were waiting. I was too weak to fight him. Salma squeezed my hand and kissed my cheek.

'Don't worry, Jacky. We are taking you to the hospital.'

* * *

Three of my ribs had been broken. A doctor and a nurse wrapped a huge stretchy bandage, which looked like a plaster, around my midriff and left me in a bed on the ward.

It was a government hospital. The ward had twenty beds and three sets of French windows opening out onto a large quad, with a long balcony running all around it. Along one wall were three very large *embubas* with a thick layer of dust covering them.

Salma stayed with me. There were no visiting hours and no catering facilities. Other patients were surrounded by women visitors, dressed in *millaya*, who had brought rugs to sit on and cassette players to listen to. Some vistors even brought Primus stoves and cooked chicken and rice for the patient right there in the ward. The windows were wide open, so that the room was swarming with flies. It was hot, sticky and uncomfortable.

'What happened?' Salma's face was a picture of concern as she stroked my hand.

'I made Omar angry again. I'll never learn,' I replied.

After three days I returned home. I had not started to bleed and the doctor had reassured me that the baby was safely growing inside me. I hadn't known whether to laugh or cry.

Once alone, Omar came into the bedroom and flung the passport on the bed.

'Thinking of leaving, were you?' he asked.

I turned my face away as he continued. 'Well, listen carefully. I will make sure that you never get the chance to try and leave me. I am taking your passport away. You will never see it again.' He grabbed my face and stared into my eyes. 'Do you understand? Never.'

'Yes, Omar.'

He released my face and paced up and down as he spoke. 'Leila is not well. She is with Mama. If you ever want to see her again, then you must never speak of what happens between us to anyone. Ever. Okay?'

'Yes, Omar.'

'You will become a good Moslem wife, who obeys her husband. I do not want to hear any more lies about my brothers. You will give me a fine son and you will stay here forever. May God forgive you for what you have done.'

'When can I see Leila?' I whispered.

'When you promise to be a good wife and never lie about my family again,' he replied.

'I promise to be a good wife. May God forgive me,' I whispered.

Satisfied, he left me alone to sleep, saying he would bring Leila home the following day.

I swung my legs over the side of the bed and went into Leila's bedroom and out onto the balcony. I looked down. We were four floors up. If I jumped, would that kill me? How could I be sure?

I stood there for a long time. 'I cannot be sure, so I cannot jump,' I told myself. I looked around the flat. 'Welcome to the rest of your life.'

28

The Outsider

The following day, I was taken to Papa's. I couldn't return to school yet. I still found it hard to breathe properly when standing for long periods and my face was a rainbow of colour.

The first person I encountered was Mohamed. He was sitting with a friend in the reception. I walked past them with my head down. He shifted uneasily on his chair, saying nothing.

Leila had a rash. As I cuddled her, she wriggled free, coughing, to toddle through to the front of the house and sit on Mohamed's knee.

I sat in the back bedroom, trying to keep my feelings under control. I didn't want Leila anywhere near Mohamed, but there was nothing I could do. What I wanted just didn't matter to anyone, I realised. Protesting certainly wasn't the answer. I would have to think of something else. For the time being I would have to keep quiet.

That evening I took Leila to the doctor's with Mama. He diagnosed German measles, proceeded to whisper in a corner with Mama and then to drop the bombshell. It was not advisable for me to keep the baby if I caught the illness from

Leila. I would have to stay away from her for two to three weeks until she had completely recovered.

Leila was my lifeline. How would I manage even another day without her? But it had been decided and there was little I could do. I bowed my head demurely and left the room, leaving Mama to look after Leila.

It took two days for the symptoms to appear: swollen glands and a slight rash. Alarmed, I returned to the doctors with Omar for reassurance. There wasn't any. I would have to lose the baby. Omar was distraught; ironic, I thought, remembering the previous week when he had laid angrily into me without a care for the baby.

Abortion was frowned upon, but available, like every other 'sin' and things considered *haram* in the Moslem world.

Somehow I expected to be taken to a little hut off the beaten track somewhere, but instead we drove to a doctor's in the centre of the city. I was led into the operating room and asked to undress behind a screen. Omar waited outside.

There was a white tin bucket, slightly rusty around the rim, half full of blood, under the bed. I lay on the bed and submitted to the anaesthetic. Fifteen minutes later it was over and I was carried, still unconscious, to the recovery room.

I came round slowly. After an hour I was able to walk, supported by Omar. And that was it. I left the building with no baby. The only thought swimming around my head was about that bucket.

'I bet it's full up now.'

* * *

I spent the next two days in bed at our flat. Omar seemed to have a change of heart, bringing me soup and drinks and taking care of himself. Mervette and Om Youssef fussed round me like mother hens, occupying Leila and giving her medicine. Mervette had no idea of what her vile husband had done. I didn't enlighten her. I was feeling delicate and desperate at the same time.

Judith and Lisa came to visit. Omar opened the door to them and was utterly charming. They had brought a get-well card signed by everyone at work. When I opened it, LE64 fell out that they'd collected in a whip round. The abortion had cost LE50 and had been paid for by Papa. This meant we could pay him back directly.

There was only a week left before the end of term and it was obvious I wouldn't be returning before then. Omar promised to take me to the school on the final day for the leaving party, to say goodbye to everyone.

After they had gone, I got up and washed the floors throughout the flat. I felt barren.

That week a pump was fitted, which gave us water in the taps. Leila's cot was finished and the workmen fitted three wall cupboards in the kitchen. Tarek walked boldly through the flat to supervise the work, without a glance at me. I played with Leila in the bedroom.

A few short months ago, I would have been literally jumping for joy. Each item individually was a step towards civilised living;

together they were a miracle. Now, I watched the developments without interest, thanking Omar with hollow smiles. I was the outsider, looking in on this life, of which I no longer felt a part.

I attended the leaving party with a heavy heart, knowing we would never see each other again. Lisa presented me with a Toshiba water heater. It should have been wonderful. Strangely, it wasn't.

I had an interview at *Madrasa Misr Lohret*, the Egyptian Language School. It was a huge, purpose-built school, providing private education for children from three to fifteen years old. It would be a very exclusive school, aimed at the rich and famous. As it was situated quite far from the affluent residential areas, fourteen buses and drivers were provided to ferry the children to and from school.

The interview was successful and I accepted the job and a place on bus number thirteen. School began at seven-thirty in the morning, which meant that the bus had to pick us up at five-thirty. With all the other stops, the journey would last one and a half hours.

In the months that followed, I assumed the role of dutiful wife and mother. Omar's moods controlled the atmosphere in the house. We spoke Arabic at all times, as did Leila. He made certain rules, within which I was free to live. I paid heavily for careless mistakes; for instance, if the food was not to his liking, or the school bus was late. He would beat me with a pole across my back, or bite me savagely on my legs. No longer did he attack my face or arms; the effects of his abuse had to pass unnoticed to the outside world.

He agreed to me having a coil fitted. This cost LE20, gave me two-week long, heavy periods, and fell out into the toilet after two months. I eventually managed to get the pill, which I took religiously.

I became very independent, visiting the *gemeier*, which was like a co-op, a government food supplier. These places received irregular supplies of food at good prices. I waited in long queues, dressed in the traditional *millaya*, covering me from head to foot, waiting to buy what was on offer: sugar, chickens, ghee, tins of tomato puree and so on. I chatted with the local shopkeepers and was now familiar with the market vendors. Leila blended in happily. Her hair was light brown and her skin fair, but she had dark brown, almond-shaped eyes that were unmistakably Egyptian. She was very close to me and I spoke English to her at school.

To all appearances I was a respectful, demure Moslem wife who fitted into the community and culture very well. The reality was very different from the impression I conveyed. The more I blended in with their ways, the more remote I felt. No matter what I did, I would always be the outsider. This wasn't me. This was an act, put on for self-preservation. But for how long could I keep it up?

My letters home were chatty, cheerful and packed with white lies. Mum and Dad were continually asking if we could visit and I made excuse after excuse. Omar would never let me out of Egypt, knowing that I would never return.

In fact, Omar seemed to have a dual personality. He was charming to visitors and friends, yet sullen and moody with me. On the one hand, he would tell me how much he loved me and we would take Leila out to the zoo or a park to play. On the other hand, he would criticise me without good reason, work himself into a rage and hit me. He began staying out, drinking beer and smoking hashish. One evening he returned just as there was a power cut. He took his frustration out on me, biting me and pushing me roughly onto the floor. As I fell, I hit the side of the chair and passed out. When I came round, he was nowhere to be seen. I went into the bedroom and was shocked to see my hair strewn over the blanket. Putting my hands up to my head, I realised that he had cut off my hair.

Even then I said nothing. It had been hacked off roughly and was many different lengths. I smartened it up as best as I could and wore a scarf.

Ramadan came and went, and Papa, although not well, made the pilgrimage to Mecca. He had saved up to make this special trip, the *hajj*, to pay homage to Allah, which all good Muslims are expected to do at least once during their lifetimes.

Leila reached her second birthday, Magda became pregnant and Tarek divorced Mervette. They had been arguing for a while over having more children. Mervette wanted to join her mother in the dressmaking business and was not ready for another child. After a huge argument lasting two days, Tarek shouted that he was divorcing her and stormed out to his mother's. Mervette poured her heart out to me. She was a beautiful, intelligent girl who wanted a bit more and she was loath to give in and have another baby.

She received her divorce through the post a few days later. It was that easy for a Moslem man to get rid of his wife: face Mecca, shout, 'I divorce you,' three times and get the appropriate form from the post office. It took another week for her mother to arrange to have the furniture removed, and they disappeared out of Tarek's life, and mine. I cried real tears for Mervette. I admired her fortitude, but I had grown to love her dearly and would miss her terribly. She had been a good friend.

My new job brought with it new friends. Nadine was an English girl, married to a rich Egyptian. They had two sons and she had converted to Islam. Her real name was Lisa, but when she changed her faith, she changed her name to Nadine. They lived in a luxurious appartment and she had a horse kept in stables near the pyramids. Nadine drove her own car, a jeep, and had the freedom to visit her friends if she wanted. I couldn't drive, let alone afford a car, so it was Nadine who visited me. She made friends with Omar and persuaded him to let Leila and me visit her once a week.

Leila loved those visits. Nadine would beep her horn, we would rush down the stairs and into the jeep, English music blaring out, and spend a couple of hours speaking English and relaxing. They ate a different sort of bread called *fino*, which was like a baguette. I had never had this in Egypt, and always chose a *fino* sandwich when she offered us lunch. She had lots of free time because her husband paid cleaners to come and do the housework and washing for her.

When the summer came, she invited us to accompany her to the stables. We spent many hours riding on the sands by the pyramids and Leila became very confident around horses. By the age of three, she was able to gallop bareback across the desert, sand flying up in her wake, holding on to the mane.

Although we were close friends, I had nothing but company to give Nadine, yet she gave me so much. I never mentioned how abusive and unpredictable my husband was. She was totally bewitched by Omar, believing him to be the perfect gentleman.

Other friends included Jill, Sally, Charlotte, Natasha and Louise, all married to Egyptians. We chatted about our lives, yet I was the only one to hide my unhappiness. As they were all well off, I could relate true stories of my poverty, without getting involved with more personal issues.

Sally, like me, was English and the youngest, at twenty-one. She had met her husband, Hussein, when he had been at university in England and she was only sixteen. They had married and settled in England, where she had given birth to a baby boy, Karim. When he was four, Hussein's parents flew over from Egypt for a three-week holiday. Returning from work one afternoon, Sally found the house empty. There was a note from Hussein to say that he had taken Karim to live in Egypt forever.

Frantic, she raised the money for the fare and flew to Egypt to reason with Hussein. He refused to hand Karim over. He no longer wanted Sally and was going to find an Egyptian wife.

Sally stayed in their house in order to be close to her son and was living in dreadful conditions, having to sleep at the foot of the bed on a rug on the floor. She had found work at the school to earn money. Hussein had married again, to a belly-dancer. They both treated her with contempt, yet she remained adamant that she would never leave until she could take Karim with her.

Charlotte, another English girl, was a beautiful, long-legged, blonde bombshell who had married an affluent Egyptian. He had travelled to Europe, was much more westernised than most husbands and was devoted to his wife. Their relationship was flourishing; there was mutual trust, he could afford to buy her gold and clothes, and take her out, and they lived in a modern flat with every convenience. Charlotte was happy and became a true friend.

Natasha was Russian. She was genuine, caring and patient. Her Egyptian husband was a lecturer, who travelled to various countries for weeks at a time. He was considerably older than she was and not a Moslem, but a Coptic Christian. They weren't particularly well off, but she had complete freedom to live as she pleased when her husband was away. To me, she was the richest of us all. She had a daughter, Sophie, who was Leila's age and they played together all the time at school.

Jill was Scottish and married to Methad, who also travelled a lot. He bought and sold gold and dealt with the jewellery shops in the Holiday Inn chain of hotels. This took him down to Luxor, to Cairo and to the Red Sea. They had two children, Jack and Sheila. They were beautiful children, with blonde hair and blue eyes, and didn't look remotely foreign. Jill made me laugh and forget the hell I was embroiled in at home.

I had been working at the school for eighteen months when Louise joined the staff. She was American, had two sons and her Egyptian husband was away a lot working. I thought she'd fit in very well. I watched her cope with her two toddlers, admiring the calm way she spoke to them.

'Whatever I do, I must never forget to take my pill,' I told myself. 'Leila is the only child I will ever have.'

That evening, at home, Omar demanded my supply of birth control pills.

'We will have a son,' was all he said as he pocketed them and left the flat.

29

My Name Is Hallah

I tried in vain to reason with Omar. By now he held my opinions in such low esteem that he refused even to listen to my pleadings. The very fact that I had questioned him made him sullen and uncommunicative for the rest of the evening. He snapped at Leila for the slightest sound she made, so that we scuttled into the bedroom to try to be quiet for him.

My acquiescence only made it easier for him to be moody and domineering. I let him get away with it. It never occurred to me to challenge him; I chose submission over violence.

I missed my period the very next month. Leila was three and a half years old by then. I saw little point in moaning about something that had been inevitable since the pills had been taken away. I told Omar with a smile, feigning delight and resigning myself to what lay ahead. He was delighted and insisted I telephone my parents with the good news.

It was a painful call, having to lie to my folks. They were happy for us and said they had sent another parcel for Leila with friends of theirs, Dave and Val Hargreaves. Mum used to send parcels regularly but we never received them. They were usually pilfered before reaching us, so she had stopped using the postal system.

The parcel arrived the following week. I didn't get the chance to meet the Hargreaves. They had delivered the parcel to the *bawab* and continued on to Alexandria where they were living. In the parcel were T-shirts, shorts and pretty hair bobbles for Leila, polo shirts for Omar, make-up and shampoo for me. Leila immediately stripped off and tried on a pair of shorts and a T-shirt. She twirled around and ran out onto the balcony, just as Omar let himself into the flat.

In a second he had grabbed her by both arms and smacked her hard on the back of her legs. She screamed, 'Mama, Mama,' wriggling to get away.

'Don't you touch her,' I said, running to free her from his grasp. Omar lashed out, hitting me on the side of my face.

'Leave us now.' His eyes bored into mine. I stood my ground, not wanting to leave Leila.

'*Rooh, Mama habibti, ana cwyaysa. Metrefeesh.*'

Leila's little eyes were imploring me to do as he said. She had told me to leave and not to worry.

I turned and went into the bedroom. Leila's screams echoed round the flat and there was a bang. I rushed out to see her crumpled on the floor crying. The shorts were torn and her legs were red from being beaten. One was bleeding from a cut.

'What on earth did he hit you with, darling?'

She looked tearfully up at me and jumped onto my knee, holding me tightly. 'His belt, Mama. He took off his belt and hit me, like he hits you. You have to burn these.'

She held out the shorts. I gently bathed the cut and read to her until bedtime. My lip had swollen up and turned purple. I sat on the bed, thoughts racing through my mind. Things were spiralling out of control. I had resigned myself to suffer the blows from Omar, but never in my wildest dreams had I considered that his bullying and beatings would spread to Leila. At three she was already wiser than her years. She had told me to leave in order to protect me, understanding that if I stayed, Papa would hurt Mama even more. What a terrible experience for my little girl to have to endure. I had to do something. But what?

I took advantage of the time spent with Nadine the following Friday to ask her about her faith. She had converted to Islam six years ago; she was very comfortable with her beliefs and how she was living out her life. I discovered that she had certain rights as a Moslem. As a foreigner and a Christian living within a Moslem community, I had no rights, even over my own daughter.

'You need to be careful,' Nadine remarked. 'If anything happens to Omar, what will you do?'

'I'd just take the first plane out of here, of course,' I replied.

'Maybe,' she replied, 'but you wouldn't be allowed to take Leila. They'd take her away from you, and if there was no further use for you, you'd be cast out of the family.'

I thought back to the day that Tarek had raped me, when I had yelled 'Scum', after him as he fled down the stairs. He was living his life as a respected member of the community, able to do anything he wanted. No. It was me who was the scum. I was nothing.

I remembered Sally, a Christian foreigner, treated like dirt, with no rights. I was no better. How could I protect Leila from anything in the future? And what of this new baby?

I returned home, resolute. We were due at Papa's for dinner that afternoon. I dressed carefully, covering my head with a long, blue chiffon scarf instead of the small square I usually tied round my head. After the washing-up, I washed my hands and carefully opened the revered copy of the Koran. Taking it through to Papa, I spent time chatting to him about the values of Islam and how I had grown to admire and respect his way of life. I explained that as a prospective mother of two, I would like to convert to Islam to be able to bring them up in an appropriate environment.

He was delighted and called the whole family in to hear the news. Lessons were arranged at the local mosque and he bought me my very own copy of the Koran in English. I was genuinely touched by his kindness and felt a pang of guilt when Salma hugged and congratulated me with tears in her eyes.

The lessons progressed throughout the summer, as did my pregnancy. After the first three months, the nausea passed and I felt healthy and well. Omar drove me to my lessons and seemed pleased with my efforts. At home, I did the specified homework and pored over the Koran, learning *suras* by heart. I began praying, chanting the *suras* in Arabic.

I finished the studies when I was eight months pregnant. Papa accompanied us to the mosque, where the imam asked me to explain the five pillars of Islam. I looked at his feet, demurely, as I replied in perfect Arabic, '*Shahadah, salat, zakat, sawm, hajj, hadritek.*'

I had addressed him with great deference. He was impressed and complimented Papa on my correct use of Arabic. I then had to explain the meanings of the pillars. I rattled the answer off with ease: there is only one God, Allah, and Mohamed is his prophet; you must pray five times a day; you must give to the poor every year; you must fast during Ramadan; you must make the pilgrimage to Mecca in your lifetime.

Papers were produced and I had to swear my faith and denounce Jesus Christ. I had to give up my Christian name and take on a Moslem name. I had chosen Hallah. Papa and I signed the certificate, and I walked out of the mosque a Moslem wife with all the rights that went with it. In the car I spread my hand over my stomach. No one could take my children away now.

I had done it. No one noticed that the name I had chosen was a palindrome. It read the same backwards as forwards.

'One day, this will be reversed and I will get my true identity back,' I resolved.

I was in favour with the family. Omar took me to a private doctor in Ahmed Orabi Street for a check-up.

'Papa wants you to have this baby in a good hospital. The doctor is excellent. His name is Ismail Hosni.'

After a thorough check-up, the doctor told me, in perfect English, that the baby was due on 18 January, in three weeks.

He asked where I worked, and suggested I take a bag with me to take to the hospital in case I started early.

The rules for maternity leave were different from England. The total number of days off allowed was fifty-seven, and they could be taken at any time, before or after the birth. I had decided to stick it out until the very last minute. I was feeling very well and I thought I would appreciate the time off when the baby arrived.

The week before I was due, Omar installed a rabbit hutch on one half of our tiny balcony. He then brought up two white rabbits and some food.

'These are for Leila,' he explained. 'To show her I love her.'

I didn't attempt to understand his reasoning. We were broke and he bought rabbits. Naturally, Leila thought they were adorable and played with them at every opportunity.

Three days later, she ran to see them after school and came running to me, screaming. They were lying dead in the hutch. They had been mutilated horribly. I shuddered, closed the shutters to the balcony and took her up to Om Youssef. She knew at once what had happened. Rats. She took us out onto her balcony, which was directly above ours and pointed to the wall of the building. Thick cracks ran all the way up from the ground. The rabbits had attracted the rats and now they would return, she informed me.

The hutch was removed and replaced with a trap, a large cage, for the rats. In the morning, I peeped round the shutter to see if we had caught one, and gasped. There were four big, grey rats pushed into the cage, going crazy to get out.

Omar picked up the cage and took it into the bathroom where he turned on the water heater. He placed the cage on the floor under the big tap and turned it on full. The rats drowned. This gruesome practice went on for days. I had to scrub the balcony every evening to try and rid it of all scent of the rabbits. Eventually they stopped coming.

My date, 18 January, came and went. I was huge by this time and wanted it to be over. When another week went by and there was still no sign, I began to think I would never give birth. Then, at work I had a few pains, but nothing really bad. This carried on through the week, with the pains starting and then stopping again. Finally, at four in the morning on 30 January, I was awoken by very strong, urgent pains. Omar rushed to find a taxi and take me to the hospital.

We arrived at five o'clock. I could hear screams from the delivery room. The doctor took one look at me and told a nurse to move the woman out, because I was further on. She emerged, flailing her arms about, screaming at the top of her voice and swearing.

'Oh my God, is it going to get as bad as that?' I thought in alarm, as the next wave of pain washed over me.

They laid me on the bed and raised both legs into stirrups. The baby was born at five-thirty precisely. Omar had promised to contact Nadine, who arrived at the same time.

There was a light system in place to let relatives know the sex of the baby. Green for a boy, red for a girl. As I pushed out my baby daughter, I passed out. In the confusion, the nurse pushed the wrong button, so that Omar and Nadine saw a green light flashing and believed the baby to be a boy.

I came round in a comfortable bed in another room. Omar was holding the baby, who had been wrapped up securely in a blanket. Nadine was holding my hand.

'You have such a wonderful husband,' she whispered. 'We were told you had a son, but then the nurse came to tell us she'd made a mistake. Your husband's face didn't alter. He just took her lovingly into his arms. You're really lucky, Jacky.'

I sat up on one elbow and watched him coo over her. A nurse appeared with an orange bowl filled with water. She took the baby and gave her a bath, finally wrapping her up and giving her to me. I snuggled her to me, feeling a rush of emotion as I touched her face with my cheek.

'Hello little one,' I whispered, burying my face into her tiny neck.

Omar put her gently into the cot at the end of the bed, kissed me and told me to rest. I was happy to oblige.

I awoke to the nurse shaking me gently. Nadine had gone. Omar was asleep in the chair. She was holding the baby out to me and asking for a tip.

I took my daughter from her and recoiled in horror. There were two strands of thick cotton protruding from her tiny ears.

'What have you done?' I asked her in Arabic.

'I've pierced her ears,' was the reply.

I looked more closely. No shiny studs or dainty earrings. This woman had pushed a needle through my baby's brand new ears and threaded cotton through them. I was horrified.

'Baksheesh?'

Now she had the cheek to ask for a tip. I launched into her, telling her she had no right whatsoever to touch my baby. She shrank back, whimpering.

Omar woke up and followed her out of the room. He calmed her down and gave her a tip.

'What's all the fuss about? Every girl has her ears pierced. It's fine.'

Leila visited with Om Youssef and Youssef. The family came and sat around the bed discussing a name. No one could agree, so we put our choices into a bag and pulled out the winner, Amira. I had wanted Yasmine, but Amira wasn't bad. It meant 'princess'.

The mother of one of my pupils came to visit me. She brought a present for Amira and placed it on the side as she left. It was a small red box. Inside was a pair of tiny, gold earrings. Mama exclaimed with delight and, within minutes, Amira had gone up in the world, from threads of cotton to threads of gold.

'My, my,' I thought to myself. 'That certainly is the work of a little princess.'

At midday, Omar helped me stand up to dress and we left the hospital. I had been there for less than eight hours. Apparently it was expensive and you paid by the hour. I was taken to Papa's, where I stayed for a whole week. Omar went to register the birth and returned waving the certificate in front of me, with the words, 'This is my insurance that you will never leave.'

I caught only a glimpse of the certificate. It meant nothing to me, covered in Arabic script. I never saw it again.

Amira was such an easy baby. She fed well, slept a lot and cried very little. She had dark brown, curly hair and green eyes, and was huge. She had weighed almost five kilos at birth.

Leila continued to go to school while I looked after Amira at the flat. I had many rich Egyptian friends through the school who sent gifts and flowers. Leila would struggle up the stairs after school, refusing to let the *bawab* help her carry the gifts from friends.

Omar continued his pretence of being the ideal husband, but behind closed doors, he often lost his temper with Leila. She would innocently incur his wrath by leaving things around. He would erupt and swing her and shake her until her shoulder would dislocate. I would then have to bundle Amira into a taxi and hold a sobbing Leila in the waiting-room until the doctor could see her. Omar always vented his rage on us and then stormed out, leaving me to pick up the pieces.

Whenever he was around, Leila changed from a happy four-year-old into an anxious, tearful girl. She had no confidence, which made her clumsy and Omar even less tolerant. Yet at school, Leila shone. She danced in a dance group to represent the school for the National Children's Festival. This was an annual event, always televised and attended by important dignitaries. After the performance, she presented a huge bouquet of flowers to the president's wife, Suzanne Mubarek. I could have burst with pride.

When Amira was eight weeks old, I returned to school. A *dada* was assigned especially to her. She was Sudanese, very black, kind and cheerful. Amira took to her straightaway.

* * *

Our lives began to improve. I started visiting Nadine once more, Leila continued to ride and I spent several afternoons at the Gezira club with Egyptian friends. Amira grew steadily, loved by so many people at the school and the family. Her curls were uncontrollable and framed her face in such a natural, attractive way. Together with her green eyes and wide smile, she attracted a lot of admirers. Parents who visited the school were always asking the *dada* who she was, and she was the darling of the drivers.

It was at Nadine's one day that I came back to earth with a bump. Leila was five and a half and Amira fifteen months. They were playing in the garden with Nadine's two boys.

'So, Jacky, Leila is growing up into a beautiful girl. Do you think she will agree to marry my son?'

I laughed. 'In your dreams, Nadine. My daughter is going to have a decent education before she thinks about marriage.'

'Is that what Omar has said? How very modern. I would have expected him to betroth her by the time she reached twelve. It's always the same with the pretty ones. Of course, he'll make her wear the veil at seven, won't he? That should keep the prying eyes off her.'

With a start, I realised that she was completely right. I had assumed that my children would have the opportunities I had had as a young girl. Here in Egypt, their lives would be over by the age of seven. It was at that moment I realised we had to get out. I had to think of something. Before Leila reached seven.

30

Secrets and Lies

This was it. I needed to get out of the country with the children as soon as possible. The problem was, I had kept everything a secret from my friends, so there was no one to confide in. I needed the moral support of at least one friend, but which one? It was vital that none of them let anything slip to their husbands. How could I decide?

The decision was taken out of my hands. That week, Louise was chatting on to me about her husband, Methad, being away so much. For the first time, she mentioned that he worked with the Holiday Inn chain of hotels.

I sat up. 'Louise, your husband works away a lot, doesn't he?'

'Yes, I've just said that.' She rolled her eyes.

'What I mean is, when Jill's husband is with her, yours is always away and vice versa?'

'And?'

'And,' I paused. 'Your husband works for the Holiday Inn chain, just like Jill's husband.'

'Does he? I don't see a lot of Jill. Our lessons are on at the same time. Maybe they know one another.'

'It would be strange if they did. Both working in the same

places. Both married to foreigners. Both called Methad.' I looked meaningfully at her, until the light began to dawn.

'Do you mean . . . could it be . . . ? But that's impossible!'

'I think we need a chat with Jill, don't you?'

It turned out that there was indeed only one Methad between them. Furious and now very wary of each other, Jill and Louise compared dates and times he was with them. Everything fell into place.

Jill sobbed and sobbed, pouring her heart out to me, her emotions swinging like a pendulum from one extreme to the other. She wanted to kill Louise. Then she wanted to kill Methad. Then she wanted to kill herself.

Finally Jill and Louise sided together against Methad, deciding that he was the rat and they had been tricked. He had made the mistake of letting them both work at the same school. For one thing, it was bound to come out sooner or later, but for another they now both knew and liked each other. It was a battle Methad could not win. Together they planned to face him with their discovery and then leave him.

The girls' optimism was short-lived. Methad announced that he was emigrating to Australia, having a job opportunity out there. He intended taking all four children with him. They were welcome to accompany him, or not. All he really wanted were his children.

After much soul-searching, both Louise and Jill decided to accompany him to be with their children. They visited the Australian Embassy to find out the regulations for emigration.

The information they were given was shocking. Australia, being a monogamous country, did not recognise polygamy. Only Methad's first wife, Louise as it turned out, would be able to accompany him. Jill would have to apply to travel to Australia in her own right.

Methad had met Louise in Luxor. He had married her and they rented a flat together. He had met Jill in Cairo. He had married her and they lived in his own house. The girls were not sure whom he had married first. They brought their marriage certificates into school the following day. The rat had actually married them within a week of each other, poor Jill just seven days after Louise.

This left Jill with her own set of problems. She was utterly devastated. We sat together every day, talking the situation over and considering the options. I decided to take the bull by the horns and confide in her about my own problems. She was brilliant. We tossed ideas between us and came to the conclusion that I needed to visit the British Embassy, while she needed the Australian one.

'You'll have to start taking things out of your flat and putting them somewhere,' she said.

'What things? And where could I put them?'

'Things that could help him to find you when you've gone. Letters from home, photos, cards. That sort of thing. Why don't you confide in Natasha? She lives in a big, old house and her husband's hardly ever there. I'm sure she'd store stuff for you confidentially.'

The enormity of what I was trying to do suddenly hit me. I

looked tearfully back at Jill. 'I don't have a passport and I don't have a birth certificate for Amira. In fact, I have nothing to prove to the world that she's even mine. Let's face it. I'll never manage to get out with the girls. Even if I could get away on my own, I wouldn't. Not without my daughters.'

Jill got up and shook me by the shoulders. 'Hey, hey, calm down. Where's your spirit gone? Now dry your eyes, we'll tell Natasha and start to plan. All you need is a good plan.'

Natasha was devastated to hear the stories of our life with Omar. Without hesitation she agreed to help in any way she could.

We began to devise ways of getting to the British Embassy without being seen. Although I had the freedom to go to the local shops or the *souk*, I could go nowhere without telling either the *bawab* or his wife exactly where I was going. Omar checked up on me daily. So far, I hadn't given him any reason to mistrust me.

The embassy was a good thirty-minute drive away, in a suburb of Cairo called Gezira. If I didn't go to school, someone would be bound to say something. So the plan was that I would take the school bus as usual and go to school, offload the girls with the *dada* and Natasha. Then I would feign a migraine and take the morning off to lie in the quiet of the medical room.

I managed three visits to the embassy in this way, slipping out and going into the city by taxi. It was a harrowing experience for me each time. My heart was in my mouth as I sat in the morning traffic. I felt much braver when Natasha and Jill were around, encouraging and supporting me. I could never have done it on my own.

At the embassy, things looked pretty bleak. I could not produce a passport and hadn't a hope of accessing Amira's birth certificate. The consul, an agreeable, middle-aged gentleman, suggested I try to locate either or both of these items to make the situation easier. He wore a pin-striped suit with a crisp white shirt and a white linen handkerchief in the top pocket of his jacket. It was wonderful to openly discuss my anxieties with someone who could actually give me the facts and tell me what I could do. Listening to the consul mulling over my case, getting straight to the point and considering possible options made me proud to be British. He didn't waste time with insincere pleasantries and didn't expect *baksheesh* to provide me with information that was rightly mine anyway. I could feel my fighting spirit returning, even though at this stage there wasn't anything concrete to fight.

I returned from the first visit very downcast, but resolute. Remembering that Karen had found her passport in the lining of Samir's wedding suit, I looked carefully through every item of clothing and under the mattress. Nothing. At Papa's I casually asked if I could see a copy of Amira's birth certificate, but was told that they didn't have it; Omar did.

When I went back to the embassy I was still empty-handed. After much discussion about the conditions I was living in and my reasons for wanting to leave, the consul agreed that my intentions were deadly serious and he sympathised with my plight. He said they could provide me with a passport in order to get back to England, but that it would not be valid for anything else. His smooth brow creased as he stressed in a worried voice that the whole operation was extremely dangerous for me. If he did produce a passport, then it would be up to me to make it valid in order to leave the country. That would mean taking it to a post office to get the required stamps and then to the main government building in Cairo for the visa. This was the difficult part. All the embassy could do was to provide the basic passport.

He looked genuinely apologetic but I quickly agreed and waited while he made a phone call. Replacing the receiver, he looked at me. 'It would, in fact, be much easier to leave Amira off the passport, since you have no proof that she is yours. Would you consider travelling with your elder daughter and then returning later for Amira?'

'It's precisely because she is my daughter that I am putting myself through this ordeal. I wouldn't exactly risk my life for someone else's child. Would you?'

I had reacted with anger and immediately realised that this wouldn't get me anywhere. I continued quickly, 'Sorry, that was uncalled for. I will do everything I can to provide you with some proof. In the meantime, could you possibly start the process of making a passport for me?'

'Of course I will.'

We shook hands and I returned to school, no one having noticed my absence.

* * *

Jill visited the Australian Embassy again. She was told that they could do nothing to help her keep her children.

'Methad can legally take his children to Australia with him. I cannot legally accompany him as his wife,' she sobbed.

'Why can't you follow him?' I asked. 'Is it a question of money?'

'No, you have to have a reason to go there and enough money. You get points for your situation when you apply and you need so many points to be accepted. Look.'

She handed me a leaflet. I scanned the list of requirements that earned points. 'Jill, let's calm down and go through this more carefully, one by one. There may be a way round this.'

Together we scrutinised the leaflet. We did in fact find a ray of hope.

'Look at this one. If you have a relative who lives there you get points. I have an uncle in Perth. Yes!' she exclaimed, throwing her arms in the air. 'This is the way I can get there.'

'You will get there. Don't give up,' I told her with a hug.

'So will you,' she replied.

I spent the days that followed putting together every scrap of evidence I had to prove who Amira was. I had a few photos at the *saboor* of the two of us, the five-piastre note with her name and date of birth on that was printed for the *saboor* and a copy of the newspaper announcement in England of her birth that my mother sent in a letter. But would it be enough?

Then, out of the blue, I had a lucky break. The Hargreaves had been back to England and had a meal with my parents.

Dave worked for Dunlop in Alexandria and he and Val lived between England and Egypt. Mum had asked them to visit and take pictures of us, particularly Amira, and deliver presents.

The day they arrived, I had just suffered a beating and Omar had stormed out, locking the door from the outside on his way. He had deliberately launched into my face, it being a holiday, knowing it would have faded by the time I returned to school.

They knocked on the door of the flat and all I could do was to open the little square in the middle of it and peer out.

Val saw me and went to say hello, but instead she took in my purple, swollen lips and half-closed eye and recoiled.

'Can I help you?' I whispered through the gap, anxious that no one could hear me talking to strangers.

Val stepped forward. 'Hi, is that you, Jacky? It's Val and Dave Hargreaves. You weren't in the last time we called.'

'Yes, I'm Jacky.' I stuffed my hand through the gap. 'Pleased to meet you both. I'm afraid you've caught me at a bad time. Omar has left the flat and locked the door, so I can't let you in.'

Dave stepped forward. 'Bad time, you say? Nasty bruise you've got there. Did he do that to you? And then lock you in?'

'Please, please keep your voice down,' I whispered urgently. 'It will only be worse for me if he knows I'm talking to you. Where did you leave your car?'

'The driver didn't want to bring it down this street after last time. It got filthy. It's on the main road.'

Another stroke of luck. I managed a lop-sided smile to myself.

'Omar has gone, but may return at any time. If you tip the *bawab* with a huge amount, say LE5 . . .'

'That's not a lot,' Dave interrupted.

'To him it is,' I assured him. 'Tell him to come and see me. There's not a lot of time, but we just may get away with it.'

'Get away with what?' Val asked.

'My plan,' I replied. 'I desperately want to get out of this hellhole, but Omar has my passport. Then there's Amira. He's got her birth certificate. The embassy have agreed to make me another passport but are reluctant to put her on because I've no proof of who she is. Would you be able to help me?'

'We'll do anything, Jacky. Just tell us what.'

'I work at the Misr Language School at Giza. If you visited me there, no one would suspect a thing. There are many foreign visitors and you would be less conspicuous. How about next Wednesday? Then we can work out what to do.'

'Does your dad know how you're treated? He never mentioned anything to us,' Dave asked.

'They think I'm happy. Why worry them?' I answered. 'Go now. Tip the *bawab* and I'll see you on Wednesday.'

Within minutes the *bawab*, usually slow and shuffling, was at my door; LE5 had obviously done wonders for his rheumatism. I told him that there was more where that money had come from if he kept quiet about the visit from the foreigners. He must tell no one, not even his wife, I told him firmly. He readily agreed and shuffled away with a smile.

He was the one weak link so far. But money talks, and I

thought such a large amount would be enough to keep his toothless mouth shut.

I waited anxiously for Omar to return. Would I get the third degree on his return? But it never happened. He arrived home with a kiss, some fresh bread and feta cheese for tea, as if that compensated for my battered face. There were no questions.

The following Wednesday, the Hargreaves visited the school. Dave had been in touch with my dad and said that I was considering leaving but had no passport or money. Dad had said that if I could manage a passport, he would telex the tickets and arrange that side of things. As far as Amira was concerned, Dave knew the vice-consul in Alexandria personally. He would have a word with him to ask what verification was needed for them to accept that Amira was my daughter. He took the school telephone number and promised to be in touch. Things had started to move.

At home, I took Leila's birth certificate and my birth and marriage certificates from the back of Leila's Baby Book. It was strange, I thought, that Omar had hidden my passport, yet not thought about the other important documents. I tucked them into my school bag to give them to Natasha for safekeeping.

A few days later, Dave telephoned to say that the consul at the British Embassy in Cairo would accept my father's word from England, if he could confirm certain details. I would then have to verify these at the same time. He had arranged for my father to ring the next morning at ten. I was expected to be there.

Fortunately it was a normal school day. With Natasha and Jill covering for me, I went to the embassy, arriving twenty minutes early and feeling extremely nervous. The consul asked me lots of questions about Amira and I gave him our certificates. My father's call came through after fifty long minutes, when I'd just about given up hope. I sat on the edge of my seat as the consul asked him questions.

Five minutes later he replaced the receiver, looked up at me and smiled for the first time. My spirits rose as he informed me that, on the basis of the information provided by my father and me, he was able to include Amira on my passport. I was required to telephone the following week to see if it was ready to be collected.

At home, I worked myself to the bone making sure everything was clean and tidy. I washed at night, hanging clothes on the balcony in the dark and bringing them in before we left for school in the morning. I washed the floors every day, spent extra time on the cooking to make sure Omar would approve. For the times when the pump was not working, I made sure there was spare water in big plastic bowls. I kept the children happy with little games or songs while I slogged. Omar visibly relaxed as I became less sullen and more attentive to him, the wife he had always wanted. He didn't suspect a thing.

It took two weeks for the embassy to produce a passport for me. I made another clandestine journey to collect it. It looked like a normal ten-year British passport: navy blue, hard-backed, except that inside it was only valid for twelve months.

The consul handed it over to me, together with my other documents.

'This is all we can do for you. Both children are included on it. If you succeed in getting out, you must renew this passport immediately.'

'Thank you,' I replied.

'It is now up to you to obtain the appropriate stamps and visas in order to leave the country. You can get the stamps at any post office, but it is normally men who do this. If they refuse to stamp it without authorisation from your husband, smile and go to another office. You must keep trying until you get them.'

'Thank you.'

'The visas are another problem. You will need patience and luck. If you succeed, then the next problem will be when you reach the Egyptian border. Again, it is not usual for a woman to leave the country unaccompanied by her husband or a male relative. If you are refused the exit visas, do not turn back.'

I looked at him, confused. 'What should I do then?'

'If you turn back, we cannot help you. Your husband will kill you. Look for another border to cross. Go on down to the Sudan. They are more lax there. But on no account turn back.'

He shook my hand warmly, sending a rush of emotion and gratitude through me. He had done so much to try and help. My eyes moistened as I told him, 'You've been so kind.'

He took his cleanly washed handkerchief from his top pocket and offered it to me. It was soft to the touch as I wiped my eyes and handed it back.

He shook his head, smiling. 'No, you keep it. Be careful. And don't come back.'

His words were ringing in my ears throughout the journey back to school. I told Natasha and Jill everything and showed them the passport.

'You've come this far, Jacky,' said Natasha, taking the passport and documents from me. 'Now let's get our heads together and plan this escape.'

31

The Execution

The very next day, during break, I strolled casually out of school down to the post office in *Shera al Haram*, Pyramid Street. I knew I would have to try quite a few, so I just approached the first counter and asked innocently what I should do in order to purchase the required stamps. My husband was away, I explained. I had lost my original passport, and this replacement had just come through.

I took a chance and looked straight into the little man's eyes, speaking perfect Arabic. I smiled innocently up at him and, as if an afterthought, produced LE5 from my purse.

'Would this be enough for someone to sort this out for me, please? My husband usually does all this kind of thing and I haven't a clue. I don't have a lot of time either, as I am a teacher at the language school and I must get back to my lessons . . .' I trailed off.

The man fell over himself to pocket the money before anyone else clapped eyes on it. Hearing me mention the prestigious school I worked at, he rushed off and ordered someone else to run around for him. He then returned to keep me company while I was waiting. I declined tea, making sure to make no further eye contact with this sweaty individual. Within fifteen minutes my passport was returned to me with the stamps inside and I was walking slowly back to school, resisting the strong urge inside me to jump for joy and race back to show the girls.

None of us could quite believe my luck. We had all been expecting much more hassle.

'It was a brilliant idea of yours for me to flirt, Jill. I did exactly as you said, just looking at him the once. Twice would have given him ideas. Once was enough to get him excited and eager to help.'

'Don't get complacent,' replied Jill. 'The hard part is yet to come. We must be sure of every detail before you try to obtain the visa. It's a long drawn-out process.'

'Yes,' agreed Natasha. 'The longer it takes, the more time Omar has to discover something. From now on you are going to have to be extra vigilant.'

'Oh, believe me, I am,' I told them. 'It's killing me and I'm completely worn out, but it's worth it.

Visas were applied for in the Mugammaa, a huge government building in Tahrir Square in the centre of the city. It had many floors, hundreds of offices and people everywhere. I was completely lost as soon as I stepped over the entrance. The noise was deafening and people brushed past me from all directions. In the taxi, I had discreetly covered myself with the traditional *millaya*. With my eyes cast down, I was just another Moslem woman to be ignored or pushed out of the way.

Boldly, I turned into the first doorway and stood in a queue.

Only it wasn't a queue, it was a mass of people pressing forward for attention at one of the numerous glass windows. They were pulling at the clothes of the people in front, waving papers around and shouting. There was no chance of me elbowing my way through, so I stood to one side to observe what exactly was going on. I was acutely aware that I only had an hour to spare; I had come during one of my free periods, when the children had music and *deen*, religion.

After a while, I was able to identify boys who were running from office to office on errands. I managed to collar a boy on his way out, tipped him with fifty piastres and asked him to take me to the appropriate office. We went up three more flights and into the right room.

A pound took me to the front of the queue, where a fat man examined my passport and asked a lot of questions. I had to shout over the noise of the crowd. When I mentioned the school, his ears pricked up and he asked me if I knew the chief of police, Hassan. I assured him that his son was in my class. I offered LE5 for a runner to help with my visas. The man stood up, came out of his booth and shook my hand. He called a runner and dispatched him into the crowds with my passport. He then asked if I could help him with his nephew's application for a place at the school. I offered to help him when my passport was ready. He thought about ten days should do it. I offered my hand in thanks and left.

I started taking little bits to school with me: a few nappies, changes of clothes, a pair of shoes. Jill packed them in a black holdall. I collected all the photo albums and letters and gave them to Natasha to store safely away. I usually kept them at the back of the wardrobe. It was unlikely that Omar would want to look at them in the coming weeks. I had to make sure that I didn't take anything that would be missed. I deliberately smashed the only framed photograph we had of me, so that I had an excuse to put the photograph in a drawer. It was transferred to Natasha a few days later.

There was very little of me left in the flat. As I scanned the rooms for any last items Omar could use later to help him find us, my gaze fell upon a photo of him in a small frame on the windowsill. I picked it up and traced the contours of his face with my finger. Tanned and smiling, his handsome features disguised the savage bully I now knew him to be.

With a sudden, almost involuntary movement, I flung the photo violently away from me and watched it turn over in the air before smashing onto the hard, stone floor. Then I calmly swept up the shards of glass and put them in the bin with the frame. Ripping the photograph into strips, making sure I tore it through the middle of his face, I struck a match and lit a burner on the cooker. The little blue flames flared up, turning orange and yellow as they ate into the tiny strips and changed them into an unrecognisable pile of ash. Satisfied, I filled the kettle and made some tea. It felt good getting rid of Omar, if only an image of him.

Jill was also making progress with her plans to go to Australia. Her uncle had provided the required invitation and she was optimistic that she would be able to get there with his help. Like everything else in Egypt, it was taking a long time.

After ten harrowing days, my nerves were at breaking point. I lived, breathed and ate our plans. I just needed that passport. If things went well, this would be my last journey into the city.

'Please God, let everything go smoothly,' I prayed, sitting in the taxi on the way to the Mugammaa.

On arrival I went straight up to the third floor. It cost me another pound to reach the glass window. The man was not there. A grim-faced, black lady in a turban sat in his place. Nevertheless I pushed my receipt through the gap with a pound note on the top. She called for a runner, who disappeared with my receipt, and indicated that I should stand aside and wait.

Ten minutes dragged by until the boy returned with three passports. One of them was navy blue. The woman glanced briefly in my direction and nodded. I pushed my way to that window, using my elbows this time. She handed it to me and was immediately occupied with her next customer.

I couldn't believe I had done it. I sat in the taxi leafing through the pages, fingering the visas, the green stamps, reading our three names. There was a sentence under the visa, written in Arabic, to say that I was married to an Egyptian national. This passport was as legal as it was going to get.

Dave Hargreaves telephoned me at the school that week. He had been busy persuading his friend, the vice-consul in Alexandria, to give him the benefit of his professional advice on the best route for me to take.

'For goodness sake don't try Cairo airport. If Omar has

hidden your passport and told you that you'll never leave, then the chances are that he has friends or acquaintances at the airport to keep a lookout if you ever did try to do a runner. It would be silly to get so far and be caught out at the airport. Also that's the first place he'll think of looking when he finds you've gone.'

'Thanks, Dave. That's good advice. So how does your friend think I should go about this?'

'Book a return bus ticket to Israel.'

'Bus? Israel? Bus?' I didn't understand. My experiences of buses to date had been a horror story. I'd landed myself in this mess in the first place because of a half-hour bus journey, and he was telling me to go all the way to Israel on one? And then come back again?

'I am speaking English, aren't I? Get someone to go to the bus station and book a ticket for the three of you. A return ticket indicates to anyone interested that you intend to return.'

'Oh, yes. That's a good idea. I see now.'

'If anyone asks why you're going to Israel, you can say that your parents are taking a holiday in Israel for two weeks. You and the girls are travelling to meet up with them for the weekend. Say you have to be back on Sunday in time to begin teaching a new week.'

I thought quickly. 'So that would mean leaving on a Friday?'

'Even better, you could leave on Thursday.'

'No, Dave. They would wonder where I was at school and alert Omar too quickly.'

'Well, you can work that part out yourself. You need bus

tickets to Tel Aviv, by the way, not Jerusalem. Your Dad will telex plane tickets through to Tel Aviv for the three of you as soon as he knows the date.'

'Okay, I'll do it your way. You've put yourself out a lot for me. Thanks.'

'I'll phone again in a couple of days to see how you're getting on. Tread carefully, Jacky. You're nearly there. Val sends her love.'

Jill, Natasha and I put our heads together to work out the finer details of the escape. We started with the plan that Dave and his friends came up with, going over every detail again and again.

'I can go to the bus station and book the tickets today,' said Jill.

'So let's go over it one more time, Jacky. What will you do when you get off the bus?' asked Natasha.

'I take a taxi to the airport or, if there's a lot of time to kill, to a hotel nearby.'

'What's your story if anyone asks why you are going straight from Israel to England?'

'Dad's had a heart attack and couldn't make the holiday. We're flying straight to England to see him in hospital.'

'Sounds good.' Jill nodded approvingly.

We eventually decided to arrange the escape for the following Thursday. Dave telephoned, as arranged, and said the tickets would be waiting for us in Tel Aviv. Mum had sent him the name of a hotel near to the airport, so I could tell the taxi driver exactly where I wanted to go.

'The flight to Heathrow will be early in the morning on Friday, so you'll need to spend Thursday night in a hotel. And whatever you do, if you're asked questions, do not deviate from your story in any way.'

'I won't.'

'Right then. Your mum and dad are waiting for you. Hang in there, Jacky. We hope to see you in England soon. Bye.'

'Goodbye, Dave. I hope so too.'

Unbeknown to Omar, I asked the bus driver not to come and collect us on Thursday. I took a day's leave of absence from work, saying that we were driving up to Alexandria for a family wedding. This was a normal thing for Egyptians to do, as weddings usually took place on a Thursday, and no one suspected a thing.

If I took Thursday off, I would not be expected back to work until Sunday. That would give me plenty of time to get a long way away.

On Wednesday at school, Natasha pressed $60 into my hand. 'In case you need hard currency at the airport. You can pay me back when I visit you in England,' she smiled.

I gave her a big hug. 'Thank you, Natasha. I love you. I'll give it to Jill to put in my bag.'

At the end of school, we said our goodbyes. I burst into tears. I couldn't help it.

'Careful, careful. You mustn't break down. Not now.'

I wiped my face on my sleeve. 'You're right. Goodbye then, you two. Take care of yourselves. And remember, don't say anything to Nadine, Sally or Charlotte until I'm out.'

I got on the bus with the girls and waved madly until they were tiny dots in the distance. At the flat I prepared our final dinner and played with the girls. Amira was worn out, so I fed her and put her to sleep. Omar came in early. We performed our prayers together and then ate. He switched on the TV while I did some washing and hung it out on the balcony.

After Leila had gone to sleep, I changed into a thin, revealing nightie I had brought with me from England. I sat on the smelly settee beside Omar and slowly and deliberately seduced him.

He was both shocked and delighted. I knew I was taking a risk in coming on to him. He could have been angry and lashed out or flattered and gone along with it. I was lucky that night, managing to keep him awake until one o'clock in the morning.

I lay awake, watching him sleep, listening to him snore. 'Sleep well, my husband. Sleep very well.'

32

The End

The hustle and bustle of the airport, once stressful and a hindrance, now dissolved into insignificance. Time seemed to stand still as I looked up imploringly into the eyes of the official.

'We have been travelling for over twenty-four hours. My father has been taken ill and is in hospital in England. We just want to make sure he is going to be all right.'

I bent down, picked up the black holdall and placed it on the desk. 'You need $4. This is all I have. Take it. There must be something inside worth $4, but please allow us to board the plane.'

Amira whined to be picked up and I obliged, plumping her on the desk beside the bag.

The official, a smart young man, looked bemusedly at the bag and then at Amira, who held out her little hand to him.

'*Lib. Ouzer lib.*'

She leaned over and stroked the lapel of his uniform, smiling her infectious smile.

He smiled back and looked questioningly at me. 'What does she want?'

'Oh, it's nothing. Excuse me. She was just asking for some

sunflower seeds. Another man in a similar uniform gave her some and she must have assumed you had some too.' I rambled on, embarrassed, and went to lift Amira off the desk.

The man intervened and picked Amira up himself. She chuckled and leant against him, crumpling his immaculate white shirt. From under the desk he brought out a paper bag containing sweets and offered one to Amira. She took one, of course, refusing to come to me.

Momentarily diverted from the ultimate problem, I was trying patiently to persuade Amira to leave the man, so that when he spoke, I wasn't really paying attention.

'It's fine, Madam. You may board the plane. We can excuse such a small amount on this occasion. There is no need to offer me your belongings.'

I stopped my cajoling and looked at him blankly. Did I hear correctly? Did he say we could go through without paying? Could it be true?

He came round the desk and placed Amira gently on the ground beside me, kneeling down to tell her to be a good girl. Leila stepped in and took Amira's hand. The man patted Leila on her head, returned to his side of the desk and handed me the black bag, smiling.

'Have an enjoyable trip. I hope you find your father in good health.'

His little excursion had given me time to come to my senses and this final sentence confirmed my wildest dreams. He was letting us go. He offered me his hand, which I shook warmly, before thanking him and moving off to the boarding lounge.

* * *

On the plane, thirty minutes later, I shook my head in wonder at what had just occurred. I had never dreamed that we would be let through; from Egypt, maybe, with a look, a lie or a bribe, but certainly not in Israel, where rules were made to be followed and spotless uniforms were meant to stay that way.

I sat between the girls, secured their seat belts and waited anxiously. For some strange reason, I was expecting Omar to burst through the door onto the plane and grab us. I gripped the arms of my seat tightly, willing the moment to arrive when the doors and hatches closed, the engines roared into life and we began to move. I examined every face of the passengers as they boarded, just to be sure, but recognised no one.

Ten minutes later, entrances and exits were sealed securely and the plane was moving slowly down the runway, preparing for take-off. It changed direction and stopped as the engines revved up with a huge crescendo. And suddenly we were racing along the runway and soaring up into the air towards the clouds and freedom.

The food was very welcome on the plane, as were the headphones. Amira ate two dinners and fell asleep. The film showing was *Crocodile Dundee*, which Leila watched, fascinated, from beginning to end.

As for me, I sat with headphones on, turned the volume down and closed my eyes. I felt dizzy thinking about the events of the past thirty-six hours. So much could have gone wrong, yet it hadn't. All those clandestine visits to the embassy and the Mugammaa, the Hargreaves' visits to our flat and the school, the stamps for the passport at the post office, the exit visas at the Egyptian border, the interrogations with the Israelis and finally the official at the airport. We had been very lucky to have come so far. I opened my eyes to make sure it hadn't been a beautiful dream and I was actually in bed at our flat. We were on a plane to London. I smiled to myself and put my arm around Leila as she watched the film. In four hours we would be walking on British soil, entering the country as British citizens.

As the plane approached London, I started to feel impatient and became fidgety. We were so close now that nothing could go wrong, could it? Suddenly the intercom crackled into life. It was the pilot, informing us that there would be a delay landing and that he would have to do a few circles in the air while we waited for other aircraft to land before us. The tension spread throughout my body as we waited. I tried to breathe deeply and calm myself, but the anticipation of landing was killing me.

Thirty minutes later we began the descent. I stared through the window in a trance, watching the trees, buildings and roads gradually grow in size and change from tiny matchbox models into reality. The wheels were released and with a jolt we were down, whizzing along the runway.

We seemed to rush along at an incredible speed, as if we would never be able to stop, but after only a couple of minutes the pilot slowed the plane right down and we were coasting gently into position at the airport. As the passengers prepared to leave, opening hatches, shouting across the aisles, pushing to get through, I slumped back into my seat. My shoulders heaved and I began to sob uncontrollably.

Leila put her hand on my knee. 'Mama?'

I could only reply with broken sentences, between my sobs. 'Don't worry, darling . . . I'm fine . . . It's just . . . I'm so . . . happy . . .'

An air hostess had noticed my distress and manoeuvred herself to our seats with a questioning look, but Leila immediately reassured her that Mama was happy, not sad.

I looked up, despite crying, and smiled through my tears. Leila was right. This was no place for tears. Quickly, I wiped my face and joined the throng of people in the aisle. We went straight through immigration without any questions.

Mum and Dad were there to meet us and resolutions were swept away in the tide of our tears. We hugged and sobbed and hugged again. We'd made it.

It took a week for Omar to even consider the possibility that we might have left the country. Natasha, my Russian friend, kept me informed with detailed letters about his movements. He had begun by visiting the school several times, chatting to the bus drivers, even threatening a few teachers he thought might be hiding something. Then he had gone to see Nadine, Charlotte and Natasha herself, whose houses he had taken me to before.

He had returned several times with a fresh set of questions, she wrote, but went away without any answers. It was the same with Charlotte, who hadn't known about my plans to escape.

After we had left and she found out, she remained a faithful friend and told him nothing. The one thing that surprised Natasha was Nadine's reaction; she had been very sympathetic towards Omar. He had been to her house crying and managed to charm his way into her heart.

Reading this only confirmed to me how right I had been in revealing my plans to only two friends. Later that week, I received a letter from Nadine, addressed to my parents' home, asking me if I was, in fact, staying with them in England. She went on to say how distressed Omar was and how he loved me so much and how sorry she felt for him . . . Why didn't I enjoy a holiday with the girls and then return to him and continue the friendship she and I had built up . . . ? Every marriage had its problems and it was the woman's job to work through them . . . she would help me . . . The final sentence made my blood run cold. She had written, 'Better the devil you know'. She had no idea.

It was with great sadness that I put Nadine's letter in a drawer. I didn't reply.

It was inevitable that the letters and phone calls would plague us. Omar rang at all times of the day and night, until Mum's nerves were at breaking point. He tried everything, from begging and declaring undying love to angry outbursts and threats of kidnap.

I immediately made both girls wards of court but, as the letters tumbled through the letterbox almost daily, worries for our safety only increased. It was the inconsistency that unnerved me more than anything else. From one letter to the next, the declarations of love became more insistent, as did the threats. He warned me that if I did not return with the girls, I would never be able to relax for even a second, because one day, he would take them away from me.

'You will have to look over your shoulder forever,' he wrote. 'Until the day you look and they are not there.'

It was a very stressful time for us. Dad began to suffer from insomnia and palpitations. They eventually decided to move house to get away from the constant unwelcome ringing of the phone and the daily arrival of post.

Even Leila was traumatised. She had put 'that other life', as she called it, away in a dark corner of her mind and did not want to talk about anything to do with Egypt. She had very little knowledge of English, yet from the day we landed in London, not a single Arabic word left her lips. She struggled to speak in English, or chose not to say anything at all. It took only two months for her to become fluent, mimicking her school friends and teachers. However, at every knock on the front door, she would shrink behind me, afraid someone might be coming to get her. It was a very long time before she would talk to any men, even if they were family friends, and if she saw a man with a beard, she would begin to cry.

In contrast, Amira continued to be a happy, unaffected little soul. She had loved life in Egypt and she loved her new life in England. Basically, she adored her big sister and as long as she was in the same room, she was content.

Four months later, Natasha and Sophie, who was also six,

flew over for a three-week visit. It was fantastic to see them. Leila was delighted to be reunited with her friend, and the more time she spent with Sophie, the more she relaxed, losing some of her anxiety.

Natasha still had no news of Jill. Louise and Methad had left for Australia with all four children and Jill was still battling with bureaucracy in order to follow them. It was too dangerous for me to contact her. I never found out what happened, but I think of her often and wonder.

Natasha also brought all my photograph albums, pictures and letters with her.

Omar's threats eventually reached the point of no return. He informed me in a letter that he had registered my 'crime' of leaving him and taking away his children with the imam. I was now a Moslem and had committed a sin against Allah and Islam. He had a fatwa issued against me. If the day arrived when he found me, he would kill me.

A year after our escape, Omar tried to get into the country with a forged invitation from me, inviting him to visit us. Fortunately the Home Office were fastidious enough to forward the letter on to me for confirmation before allowing him entry, so his plan was thwarted. Gradually we lost contact.

And so I am writing fifteen years on, still in England, still with my daughters. I could never live my life under the maxim, 'Better the devil you know'. If I had the chance to risk everything again for the sake of what I believed in, I would do it all over again. It has taken all these years to acquire a passport for Amira, her birth certificate buried somewhere in one of the many registry offices in Cairo. At eighteen, she can finally travel, drive and get married if she wishes, because that passport gives her an identity and the freedom to do those things.

I wrote this book for two main reasons. The first was in order to document the events that led to the birth of my daughters and the reasons for our escape. Leila and Amira have never really asked much about it. There will come a day when they want to know more. This is more.

The second reason was to send a strong message to all you romantics out there who meet a handsome foreigner and fall head-over-heels in love with him. Beware! Read my story and think about the big picture. If I stop just one of you running off into a foreign sunset, then for me the book has been worth it.

The fatwa still dominates my life, although none of my colleagues or acquaintances would ever know. I still look over my shoulder, every day. I always will.

Acknowledgments

I am blessed with a few good friends who have supported me throughout this weird, energy-charged, frenzied period, reading, evaluating and supporting me along the way. Lisa, Karen and Liz, I love you.

My wonderful mum gave me her all, encouraging me and struggling to listen to parts of chapters, having a huge battle of her own with cancer. She lost that battle only three months ago. Mum, thank you.

But for Dave and Val, I would not be sitting here today. My story would be a far cry from these pages. I will always be grateful.

My MP, Mr Austin Mitchell, fought for a long time to locate my daughter Amira's birth certificate, although in vain. His efforts were paramount in our being able to obtain a passport for her when she reached the age of eighteen. I appreciate this very much.

There is a lady who works in the passport office, who has supported me for years, as I tried in vain to obtain an identity for Amira in the form of a passport. After many attempts, she eventually advised me to wait until Amira reached eighteen, when she could apply in her own right, with no obligation to inform her natural father. Two days before Amira's eighteenth birthday, she cared enough to telephone me at home to say that the passport would be issued on her birthday. She would crack a bottle at home to celebrate, and would I be doing the same? Through my tears, I confirmed that I would be doing exactly that. Her name is Christine Macmillan.

I am also indebted to my editor, Clifford Thurlow, who has taught me so much. His patience, support and gentle guidance have given me the confidence to let my pen literally fly across the pages, culminating in my book, of which I am very proud.

Finally, my two beautiful daughters have been my inspiration and my reason for carrying on. Thank you.